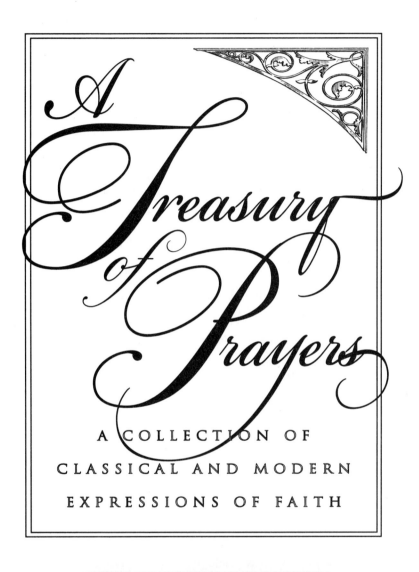

A Treasury of Prayers

A COLLECTION OF CLASSICAL AND MODERN EXPRESSIONS OF FAITH

STEVE FORTOSIS

kregel
PUBLICATIONS

Grand Rapids, MI 40501

A Treasury of Prayers: A Collection of Classical and Modern Expressions of Faith

© 2001 by Steve Fortosis

Published by Kregel Publications, a division of Kregel, Inc., P.O. Box 2607, Grand Rapids, MI 49501. Kregel Publications provides trusted, biblical publications for Christian growth and service. Your comments and suggestions are valued. For more information about Kregel Publications, visit our Web site: www.kregel.com.

Library of Congress Cataloging-in-Publication Data
  A treasury of prayers: a collection of classical and modern expressions of faith / [compiled] by Stephen Fortosis.
      p.   cm.
  Includes bibliographical references and index.
  1. Prayers. I. Fortosis, Stephen.
BV245 .T68   2001   242.8—dc21   2001023438
                                        CIP
ISBN 0-8254-2642-1

Printed in the United States of America

1 2 3 4 5 / 05 04 03 02 01

Christmas 2003

To my dad
who knew God as his closest friend
and who always wanted to pray with me.

Dear Mom,

I Love you so much!
Thank you for all you have
Done for me and all of the
Love you have shown me for all
my life! you have always been
the best mom and I Love you
dearly for it. You have taught me
so much about life, love, and God!
Thank you for all of your knowledge
and love and humor and compassion.
I Love you and I will always
Cherish all our special
moments we have had and
our special moments to come.

Love,
Kes

More things are wrought by prayer than this world dreams of;
Wherefore, let thy voice rise like a fountain for me night and day.
For what are men better than sheep or goats
That nourish a blind life within the brain.
If, knowing God, they lift not hands of prayer
Both for themselves and those who call them friends,
For so the whole round earth is every way
Bound by gold chains about the feet of God.
—Alfred Lord Tennyson

Contents

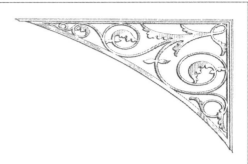

Introduction

Father, the world doesn't know quite what to think about prayer. I heard a radio listener tell a DJ that she'd be praying for him. He replied, "Well, that's nice. I appreciate all your good thoughts." Good thoughts? Is that all prayer is? A pragmatic habit—a ploy to engage the power of positive thinking?

I read about a research study in which some hospital patients were prayed for daily and others were not. At the end of the study, most of the patients who had been prayed for were in better condition and in better spirits.

Lord, some think of prayer as designed only for crisis. People turn to You in tragedy, at funerals, in foxholes. They think, *It sure couldn't hurt to call on God in times of trouble. And it* does *make one feel better.*

Most of us don't pray often or consistently. Life is too short, after all, to spend time sitting around praying. We say, "I have to survive," or "People demand too much of my time," or "By the time I stop to pray, I'm so tired that I just doze off."

Also, God, we're so used to entertainment . . . and prayer isn't entertainment. Sometimes it even feels like work. We often just don't feel like praying. We don't know how to express the crazy emotions inside. We think we need to be eloquent . . . or at least able to make sense.

We get tired of praying for the same needs over and over. Talking to You becomes mechanical. And You know how hard it is for us sense-oriented creatures to talk to someone whom we can't see, can't audibly hear, or can't touch. At times, it feels like we're talking to ourselves or to the ceiling.

Lord, please help us to pray wisely and often, and with a real sense of Your presence. Lord, please reveal Yourself to us as we pray, and may we converse with You as we do with our closest intimates. You know some of us are people of few words; please understand that we don't talk to *anyone* in an endless flow of words. And for those of us who love to talk, overlook the times we go off on endless tangents in our prayers.

We do love You, God. As poorly and inconsistently and hypocritically as we humans sometimes love, please know that we want to love You as You deserve. This book contains the deepest heart cries of your people—the candid, stumbling prayers of young and old. Teach us all we can learn from the conversations others have had with You—You, who are the greatest and the best. We want to learn.

1

Prayers in Crisis

God, you know how hard this is for me. My heart is breaking. Juliann is not going to make it. As her mother, I do not
have the courage and strength to give her back to you right
now. Please give me your courage and strength. Hold me,
Father, I come as a little child wanting to crawl up onto
your lap and just be held. I cannot walk this road alone.
Lord, I want your will for her life, whatever that may be.[1]
—Sheri Bignell

Sheri uttered this prayer as, in a hospital, her five-year-old
daughter's life slipped away after she had choked on a seizure
medication.

O LORD, God of our fathers, are you not the God who is in
heaven? You rule over all the kingdoms of the nations. Power
and might are in your hand, and no one can withstand you.
O our God, did you not drive out the inhabitants of this
land before your people Israel and give it forever to the de-
scendants of Abraham, your friend? . . .

But now here are men from Ammon, Moab, and Mount
Seir, whose territory you would not allow Israel to invade
when they came from Egypt; so they turned away from them
and did not destroy them. See how they are repaying us by
coming to drive us out of the possession you gave us as an

inheritance? O our God, will you not judge them? For we have no power to face this vast army that is attacking us. We do not know what to do, but our eyes are upon you.

—King Jehoshaphat
2 Chronicles 20:6–12 NIV

This battle was won. As those in Judah sang praises, the disparate enemy forces turned against each other, annihilating one another's armies.

Once again, our Father, the long weekend that brings rest and refreshment to so many of our people has brought disaster and sorrow to some, and our nation is sobered in the reflection that death is in the midst of life. Since we know not at what moment the slender thread may be broken for us, teach us to number our days that we may apply our hearts unto wisdom. And may we be compassionate, remembering the hearts that are sore and our brethren who languish in sorrow and affliction.

Take from us the selfishness that is unwilling to bear the burdens of others while expecting that others shall help us with ours. Make us so disgusted with our big professions and our little deeds, our fine words and our shabby thoughts, our friendly faces and our cold hearts, that we shall pray sincerely this morning for a new spirit and new attitudes. Then shall our prayers mean something, not alone to ourselves but to our nation. In the name of Jesus Christ our Lord.[2]

—Peter Marshall

Peter Marshall served for several years as the chaplain for the United States Senate. The prayer above was prayed in the Senate after a tragic Memorial Day weekend in 1947: in Japan, an Army C-54 rammed into a mountain; in Iceland a DC-3 crashed; at LaGuardia Field, New York, a DC-4 was annihilated; and on June 2, another DC-4 fell into a Maryland bog. Total casualties—160.

When I see you in heaven I shall be filled with joy, and you will give me rest. I shall no longer have to live in this world

and watch my people suffering, your churches destroyed, your altars overthrown, the weak abused. . . .

Yet I intend to remain firm in my faith, and to walk bravely along the path which you have marked out for me. . . . You will allow me to lead my brethren into that life in which there are no cares, no anxieties; where there is neither persecutors or persecuted, neither oppressor nor oppressed, neither tyrant nor victim.

This day, the day of my death, I shall not stumble as I walk the way you have set before me because you shall hold me up. My weary limbs will find strength in you, and the grief in my heart will be forgotten. . . . You will wipe away the tears from my eyes and fill me with joy.[3]

—Simon the Persian

The above is an excerpt from a prayer offered by Simon before he was burned at the stake, A.D. 339.

Take my hand, Precious Lord,
Lead me on, let me stand.
I am tired, I am weak, I am worn.
Through the storm, through the night, lead me on to the light.
Take my hand, Precious Lord, lead me home.

When my way grows drear, Precious Lord, linger near
When my life is almost gone.
Hear my cry, hear my call, hold my hand, lest I fall.
Take my hand, Precious Lord, lead me home.

When the darkness appears and the night draws near
And the day is past and gone,
At the river I stand,
Guide my feet, hold my hand.
Take my hand, Precious Lord, lead me home.[4]

—Thomas Dorsey

O God, give us patience when the wicked hurt us. O how impatient and angry we are when we think ourselves unjustly slandered, reviled and hurt! Christ suffers strokes upon his cheek, the innocent for the guilty; yet we may not abide one rough word for his sake. O Lord, grant us virtue and patience, power and strength, that we may take all adversity with good will and with a gentle mind overcome it. And if necessity and your honour require us to speak, grant that we may do so with meekness and patience, that the truth and your glory may be defended, and our patience and steadfast continuance perceived.[5]

—Miles Coverdale

Coverdale was exiled during the reign of Mary Tudor, in part because he translated the Bible into the English of his day.

O Lord God, when Thou givest to Thy servants to endeavor any great matter, grant us also to know that it is not the beginning, but the continuing of the same, until it be thoroughly finished, which yieldeth the true glory; through Him that for the finishing of Thy work laid down His life, our Redeemer, Jesus Christ.[6]

—Sir Francis Drake

This prayer was composed by Sir Francis Drake on the morning he sailed into the Bay of Cadiz to face his enemies.

Lord, save me!

—Simon Peter
Matthew 14:30 NIV

Peter beseeched rescue when he walked upon water then began to sink.

Dear Master of the Wind and Waves, help me when the sudden storms of life come crashing over me with their fierce winds and frothing waves. I have seen enough storms, Lord, to know how quickly peaceful circumstances can turn into catastrophe.

I have seen the strong become weak with disease. I have seen the freest of spirits become enslaved with addiction. I have seen the brightest of stars fall like meteors in a streak of dying fame.

I have seen respected preachers and politicians disgraced to become the laughingstocks of the land.

I have seen banks go bankrupt, their riches taking wings on the updrafts of plummeting markets. I have seen fortunes lost in gold, silver, and precious stones. I have seen dynasties of oil, real estate, and stocks swept overboard to the bottom of the sea.

I have seen the faithful lose faith. I have seen happy marriages with hopeful beginnings end up on the rocks of infidelity. And I have seen prodigals blown off course to sink in a sea of sin.

Yes, Lord, I have seen a lot of storms. Too many of other people's to feel untouchable. Too many of my own to feel critical or proud or unsympathetic.

Some dear people I love, Lord, are going through some tempestuous times right now. Help them to see you in the midst of their storms—you who rule the wind and waves with only a word. And help them to see that no matter how devastating the storm that sweeps over them, you do care if they drown. Help them not to be hasty in judging your concern for them during those times when their lives seem to be sinking and you seem to be asleep in the stern.

Help them to see that you allow storms in their lives to strengthen them—not to shipwreck them. And help them to see that it is you who not only points out the direction their lives should take but who rides with them to hasten their safe passage.

Thank you, Lord Jesus, for being there during their individual storms. And when uncertain seas unsettle their faith, turn their attention to you so that the tempest in their souls might be quieted and made still.[7]

—Ken Gire

Father, It is better to die for Jesus than to rule over the ends of the earth. . . . I am God's wheat. May I be ground by the teeth of the wild beasts until I become the fine wheat bread that is Christ's. My passions are crucified, there is no heat in my flesh, a stream flows murmuring inside me; deep down in me it says: Come to the Father.[8]

—Ignatius of Antioch

Ignatius offered this prayer before he faced lions in a Roman arena, A.D. 107.

Gracious Father in heaven, our hearts unite with all people in profound gratitude that the life of the President of the United States was spared. We pray for his rapid and complete recovery. We commend to Thy loving care Mrs. Reagan and the family. May the peace which passes understanding fill their hearts and minds.

We pray for total recovery for Mr. Brady, Mr. McCarthy, and Mr. Delahanty. Grant the healing touch of the Great Physician in their lives and the comfort and peace of His presence with their loved ones.

We thank Thee for the Secret Service and the police and all who provide security at the risk of their lives. For the Vice President and all in authority, we pray for Thy guidance and direction through these crucial hours; and for our nation, we pray that we may persevere to Thy glory.

We have been vividly reminded how transitory life is. May we, therefore, conduct ourselves in the wisdom of James, who wrote, "What is your life? For you are a mist that appears for a little time and then vanishes" (James 4:14 RSV).

Hear our prayer in the name of the Lord Jesus Christ.[9]

—Richard Halverson, Chaplain
United States Senate

Halverson presented this prayer after President Reagan was shot.

Lord,
Thou knowest I shall be verie busie this day;
I may forget Thee;
Do not Thou forget me.[10]
—Baron Jacob Astley
Before the Battle of Edgehill, 1643

Father in heaven, you who have forgiven man in the past, forgive these men also. Do not let them perish in their sins but bring them into yourself.[11]
—Kefa Sempangi

Five of Idi Amin's hit men were sent to murder Pastor Sempangi. When asked if he had any last words, the pastor said he would pray for the assassins. The gang leader asked, "Will you pray for us now?" After the above prayer, the five men left the church without causing harm, and the gang leader later became a Christian.

O Lord Almighty, God of Israel, enthroned between the cherubim, you alone are God over all the kingdoms of the earth. You have made heaven and earth. Give ear, O Lord, and hear; open your eyes, O Lord, and see; listen to all the words Sennacherib has sent to insult the living God.

It is true, O Lord, that the Assyrian kings have laid waste all these peoples and their lands. They have thrown their gods into the fire and destroyed them, for they were not gods but only wood and stone, fashioned by human hands. Now, O Lord our God, deliver us from his hand, so that all kingdoms on earth may know that you alone, O Lord, are God.
—King Hezekiah
Isaiah 37:16–20 NIV

When Jerusalem was besieged by the Assyrian army, Hezekiah received a letter from Sennacherib and read it. Then he went up to the

temple of the Lord, spread the letter out before the Lord, and spoke the prayer above.

> O Lord, great distress has come upon me; my cares threaten to crush me, and I do not know what to do. O God, be gracious to me and help me. Give me strength to bear what you send, and do not let fear rule over me. . . . Whether I live or die, I am with you, and you, my God, are with me. Lord, I wait for your salvation and for your kingdom.[12]

—Dietrich Bonhoeffer

This pastor and theologian was executed by the Nazis at Flossenburg concentration camp at dawn on April 9, 1945.

> Lord, have mercy on me; all day long the enemy troops press in. So many are proud to fight against me; how they long to conquer me.
>
> But when I am afraid, I will put my confidence in you. Yes, I will trust the promises of God. And since I am trusting him, what can mere man do to me? They are always twisting what I say. All their thoughts are how to harm me. They meet together to perfect their plans; they hide beside the trail, listening for my steps, waiting to kill me. They expect to get away with it. Don't let them, Lord. In anger cast them to the ground.
>
> You have seen me tossing and turning through the night. You have collected all my tears and preserved them in your bottle! You have recorded every one in your book.
>
> The very day I call for help, the tide of battle turns. My enemies flee! This one thing I know: God is for me! I am trusting God—oh, praise his promises! I am not afraid of anything mere man can do to me! Yes, praise his promises. I will surely do what I have promised, Lord, and thank you for your help. For you have saved me from death and my feet from slipping, so that I can walk before the Lord in the land of the living.

—David
Psalm 56 LB

This was David's prayer when Philistines seized him in Gath and he feared for his life.

> Gracious God, Lord of life, forty-six hours ago, cosmic tragedy galvanized America into one united family as seven valiant pioneers were taken from us.
>
> In profound silence, as though life was in suspension, millions watched in unbelief and waited transfixed, hoping against hope. For those unforgettable moments, perhaps hours, we were all one in shock and grief—all races, all ages, the high and mighty, the low and weak—all one in inexpressible agony, with an overwhelming sense of loss.
>
> We thank You for the greatness of the American heart revealed in the strong and tender response of our leadership, the reassuring, healing message of the President, the instinctive resort to prayer of the Congress, the compassionate words of senators and representatives, the emerging conviction that the sacrifice of the heroes was not in vain, but rather stimulus to national renewal of our commitment to space.
>
> Thank you, Almighty God, for the seven heroes, their families, our leaders, the people of American, and the sensitive coverage by the news media.
>
> Praise God for America.[13]
>
> —Richard Halverson, Chaplain
> United States Senate

Chaplain Halverson offered this prayer following the Challenger tragedy, January 28, 1986.

> Dear God, I was watching TV when the Challenger shuttle exploded. That was a sad thing. Was there anything you could have done? Were you mad because they came too close to your territory?
>
> We're sorry.[14]
>
> —José [age 11]

Oh my God, thou hast caused me to be born at a time and hour ordained by thee. During all the days of my life thou hast guarded and preserved me through great dangers and hast delivered me from them all. And now, when the time has come that I must pass from this life to thee, then thy good will be done. I cannot escape from thy hands. And if I could, I would not, for it is my joy to conform to thy will.[15]

—Guido de Bres

De Bres was a Reformer, who wrote thirty-seven articles of faith in 1561 as the Belgic Confession. Many scholars today call this one of the best written expressions of Christian faith of all time.

De Bres uttered the prayer above while imprisoned in a Doornik castle. At six A.M. on May 31, 1567, he was hanged for his faith. In his quiet farewell to fellow prisoners, he said, "Brothers, this morning I have been condemned to death for the doctrine of the Son of God. Praise be to him. I am happy. I never dared to think that God would do me such an honor."

Lord, the motor under me is running hot. There are twenty-eight people and lots of luggage in the truck. Underneath are my bad tires. The brakes are unreliable. Unfortunately I have no money—parts are difficult to get. And Lord, I did not over-load the truck.

Lord, "Jesus is mine" is written on the vehicle, for without him I would not drive a single mile. The people in the back are relying on me. They trust me because they see the words, "Jesus is mine." Lord, I trust you!

First comes the straight road with little danger; I can keep my eyes on the women, children, and chickens in the village. But soon the road begins to turn, it goes up and down, it jumps and dances, this death-road to Kumasi. Tractors carrying ma-hogany trunks drive as if there were no right or left. Lord, Kumasi is the temptation to take more people than we should. Let's overcome it!

The road to Accra is another problem. Truck drivers try to beat the record—although the road is poor and has many holes

and there are curves before we come to the hills. And finally to Akwasim. Passing large churches in every village, I am reminded of You, and in reverence I take off my hat.

Now downhill in second gear.[16]

                     —A prayer from Ghana, W. Africa

Dear God, out of necessity the announcement was casual. How else can a doctor break the news, "You have a tumor"? Momentarily my world was shattered. Outwardly there were few signs . . . , but inwardly things began to churn. I had promised to go to a luncheon, but how should I act? As if nothing had happened?

The doctor urged me to go to the hospital immediately. I told him I couldn't! I had plans and commitments. We compromised. I would fulfill some major commitments and then check into the hospital.

On Monday we headed for the hospital. The examination by a specialist there confirmed the doctor's suspicion—it was a malignant tumor. Now, three days later . . . I'm to be operated on. You have consistently covered me with the wings of your Spirit! I've had my dips, but always underneath were your everlasting arms.

Now I want to witness to what it means to trust you in such a time. I want to tell the world what freedom there is in being able to say, "Whether I live or die, I am the Lord's." I love life, Lord, and if you should give me more time, I would want to be about your business. But God, if this is the time you tap me on the shoulder, what anticipations are mine! Sometimes I try to imagine the beauty and wonder of it. You've told us that it's beyond human comprehension and your Son has shown us the way. . . . He said, "Whoever believes in me will live, even though he dies."

Thank you for your forgiveness! I'm ready, Lord, for whatever tomorrow might hold. Precious Lord, take my hand.[17]

                     —Ruth Youngdahl Nelson (excerpted)

Ruth was voted Mother of the Year in 1973.

2

Prayers of Praise and Worship

All you big things, bless the Lord.
Mount Kilimanjaro and Lake Victoria,
The Rift Valley and the Serengeti Plain,
Fat baobabs and shady mango trees,
All eucalyptus and tamarind trees,
Bless the Lord. Praise and extol Him forever and ever.

All you tiny things, bless the Lord.
Busy black ants and hopping fleas,
Wriggling tadpoles and mosquito larvae,
Flying locusts and water drops,
Pollen dust and tsetse flies,
Millet seeds and dried dagaa,
Bless the Lord. Praise and extol Him forever and ever.[1]
                              —Traditional African verse

The prayers I make will then be sweet indeed
If Thou the spirit give by which I pray.
My unassisted heart is barren clay,
That of its native self can nothing feed,
Of good and pious works Thou art the seed

That quickens only where Thou say'st it may.
Unless Thou show to us thine own true way
No man can find it: Father! Thou must lead.
Do Thou, then, breathe those thoughts into my mind
By which such virtue may in me be bred,
That in Thy holy footsteps I may tread;
The fetters of my tongue do Thou unbind
That I may have the power to sing of thee
And sound Thy praises everlastingly.[2]

—Michelangelo Buonarroti

O Thou, who art the ever-living Lord, we acknowledge how weak and finite we are, for we know that we are all tending toward inevitable decay and the final moment of our lives, and we sometimes tremble at the unknown Beyond. But to-day our fears are hushed and our hopes triumph as we join the Apostles and the saintly women in the glad wonder of Easter. We bless Thee for the disk of rock revolving in its groove, the opened tomb, the King in His beauty walking among the lilies of the garden, the women in an ecstasy of surprise and joy, the disciples racing to the tomb and finding it untenanted by the shrouded form that lay upon its rocky shelf.

The resurrection of the Redeemer! Christ, the first fruits, and afterward they that are Christ's at his coming—the waving of the single sheaf before the Lord, pattern and pledge of the glorious human harvest which shall one day wave over all the fields of God. May all the bewildered sorrowing and desolate wrap the Easter thought around their sore and weary hearts so that cold and cheerless habitations may glow with warmth; that the "empty chair" may somehow lose its power to depress; that no one may have any dread of taking the returnless path himself, but comfort and calm may displace sorrow, and courage and peace may expel fear. "Therefore let us be steadfast, unmovable, always abounding in the work of the Lord, forasmuch as we know that our labor is not in vain in the Lord."[3]

—Frederick Lewis

Thy home is with the humble, Lord,
  The simple are Thy rest;
Thy lodging is in childlike hearts;
  Thou makest there Thy nest.[4]
              —F. W. Faber

No voice of prayer to Thee can rise,
But swift as light Thy love replies;
Not always what we ask, indeed,
But, O most Kind, what most we need.[5]
              —H. M. Kimball

You are the great God—He who is in heaven.
You are the creator of life, you make the regions above.
You are the hunter who hunts for souls.
You are the leader who goes before us.
You are he whose hands are with wounds.
You are he whose feet are with wounds.
You are he whose blood is a trickling stream.
You are he whose blood was spilled for us.[6]
       —Anonymous prayer of a Xhosa Christian
                       in South Africa

O Lord our God! You know who we are: men with good consciences and with bad, persons who are content and those who are discontent, the certain and the uncertain, Christians by conviction and Christians by convention, those who believe, those who half-believe, those who disbelieve. . . .

But now we all stand before you, in all our differences, yet alike in that we are all in the wrong with you and with one another, that we must all one day die, that we would all be lost without your grace, but also in that your grace is promised and made available to us all in your dear Son, Jesus Christ. We are here together in order to praise you through letting you speak to us. We beseech you to grant that this may take place in this hour, in the name of your Son our Lord.[7]
                                    —Karl Barth

When the Nazis began to gain power, Barth was removed from teaching theology because he moved from neutrality to an active involvement with the Confessing Church, which openly opposed Hitler and remained loyal only to Christ. When Barth refused to take an oath of obedience to Hitler, he was exiled to his native town.

> Lord of all being, throned afar,
> Thy glory flames from sun and star;
> Centre and soul of every sphere,
> Yet to each loving heart how near!
>
> Sun of our life, thy quickening ray
> Sheds on our path the glow of day;
> Star of our hope, thy softened light
> Cheers the long watches of the night.
>
> Our midnight is thy smile withdrawn,
> Our noontide is thy gracious dawn,
> Our rainbow arch thy mercy's sign;
> All, save clouds of sin, are thine.
>
> Lord of all life, below, above,
> Whose light is truth, whose warmth is love,
> Before thy ever-blazing throne
> We ask no lustre of our own.
>
> Grant us thy truth to make us free
> And kindling hearts that burn for thee,
> Till all thy living altars claim
> One holy light, one heavenly flame.[8]
> —Oliver Wendell Holmes

Come forth out of Thy royal chambers, O Prince of all the kings of the earth; put on the visible robes of Thy imperial majesty, take up that unlimited sceptre which Thy Almighty Father hath bequeathed Thee, for now the voice of Thy bride calls Thee, and all creatures sigh to be renewed.[9]
—John Milton

O Lord, Thou hast searched me, and known me.

Thou knowest my downsitting and mine uprising, thou understandest my thought afar off.

Thou compassest my path and my lying down, and art acquainted with all my ways.

For there is not a word in my tongue, but, lo, O Lord, thou knowest it altogether.

Thou hast beset me behind and before, and laid thine hand upon me.

Such knowledge is too wonderful for me; it is high, I cannot attain unto it.

Whither shall I go from thy spirit? or whither shall I flee from thy presence?

If I ascend up into heaven, behold thou art there: if I make my bed in hell, behold, thou art there.

If I take the wings of the morning, and dwell in the uttermost parts of the sea;

Even there shall thy hand lead me, and thy right hand shall hold me.

If I say, Surely the darkness shall cover me; even the night shall be light about me.

Yea, the darkness hideth not from thee; but the night shineth as the day: the darkness and light are both alike to thee. . . .

How precious also are thy thoughts unto me, O God! how great is the sum of them!

If I should count them, they are more in number than the sand: when I awake I am still with thee. . . .

Search me, O God, and know my heart: try me and know my thoughts:

And see if there be any wicked way in me, and lead me in the way everlasting.

—David
Psalm 139 KJV

As flame streams upward, so my longing thought
  Flies up with Thee,
Thou God and Savior, who hast truly wrought
Life out of death, and to us, loving brought
A fresh, new world; and in Thy sweet chains caught
  And made us free.[10]

      —Maurice Egan

  Be quiet, why this anxious heed
  About my tangled ways?
  You know them all, You giveth speed,
  And You allow delays.[11]

      —E. W. (adapted)

    Rest of the weary,
    Joy of the sad,
    Hope of the dreary,
    Light of the glad;
    Home of the stranger,
    Strength to the end,
    Refuge from danger,
    Savior and Friend.

    Pillow where, lying,
    Love rests its head;
    Peace of the dying,
    Life of the dead;
    Path of the lonely,
    Prize at the end;
    Breath of the holy,
    Savior and Friend.

    When my feet stumble
    I'll to Thee cry;
    Crown of the humble,
    Cross of the high,
    When my steps wander,

Over me bend,
Truer and fonder,
Savior and Friend.

Ever confessing
Thee, I will raise
Unto Thee blessing,
Glory and praise;
All my endeavor,
World without end,
Thine to be ever,
Savior and Friend.[12]
—J. Monsell

How simple for me to live with you, Oh Lord. How easy for
me to believe in you! When my mind parts in bewilderment
or falters, then the most intelligent people see no further than
this day's end and do not know what must be done tomorrow. You grant me the serene certitude that You exist and that
You will take care that not all the paths of good be closed.
Atop the ridge of earthly fame, I look back in wonder at the
path which I alone could never have found, a wondrous path
through despair to this point from which I, too, could trans-
mit to mankind a reflection of your rays. And as much as I
must still reflect You will give me. But as much as I cannot
take up You will have already assigned to others.[13]
—Alexander Solzhenitsyn

Thou hidden Source of calm repose,
   Thou all-sufficient Love divine,
My help and refuge from my foes,
   Secure I am, if Thou art mine;
And lo! from sin, and grief, and shame,
   I hide me, Jesus, in Thy name.

Jesus, my all in all Thou art,
   My rest in toil, my ease in pain,

The medicine of my broken heart—
   In war my peace, in loss my gain,
My smile beneath the tyrant's frown,
   In shame my glory and my crown.

In want my plentiful supply,
   In weakness my almighty power;
In bonds my perfect liberty,
   My light in Satan's darkest hour,
My joy in grief, my shield in strife,
   In death my everlasting life.[14]
               —Charles Wesley

Hail, sovereign Love, which first began
The scheme to rescue fallen man.
Hail, matchless, free, eternal grace,
Which gave my soul a hiding place.

Against the God that built the sky
I fought with hands uplifted high—
Despised the mention of his grace,
Too proud to seek a hiding place.

Ere long a heavenly voice I heard,
And mercy's angel soon appeared;
He led me, with a beaming face,
To Jesus as my hiding place.

Should sevenfold storms of thunder roll,
And shake this globe from pole to pole,
No thunderbolt shall daunt my face,
For Jesus is my hiding place.[15]
               —Major Andre

Major Andre was executed later as a spy during the American Revolution.

Full of glory, full of wonders, Majesty Divine;
Mid Thine everlasting thunders
How Thy lightnings shine.
Shoreless ocean, who shall sound Thee?
Thine own eternity is round Thee, Majesty Divine.

Timeless, spaceless, single, lonely,
Yet sublimely Three,
Thou art grandly, always, only, God in unity,
Lone in grandeur, lone in glory,
Who shall tell Thy wondrous story, Awful Trinity?

Thine own Self forever filling with self-kindled flame,
In Thyself Thou art distilling unctions without name.
Without worshipping of creatures
Without veiling of Thy features, God always the same.

'Mid Thine uncreated morning, like a trembling star,
I behold creation's dawning, glimm'ring from afar;
Nothing giving, nothing taking,
Nothing changing, nothing breaking,
Waiting at time's bar.

Splendors upon splendor beaming—change and intertwine;
Glories over glories streaming, all translucent shine.
Blessings, praises, adorations,
Greet Thee from the trembling nations
Majesty Divine![16]

—F. W. Faber

Lord, with what courage and delight
  I do each thing,
When Thy least breath sustains my wing;
  I shine and move
  Like those above,
  And, with much gladness
  Quitting sadness,
Make me fair days of every night.[17]
—H. Vaughan

A broken *altar*, Lord, thy servant rears,
Made of a heart, and cemented with tears:
  Whose parts are as thy hand did frame;
  No workman's tool hath touched the same.
    A *heart* alone
    Is such a stone,
    As nothing but
    Thy pow'r doth cut.
    Or my hard heart
    Meets in this frame,
    To praise thy name.
  That, if I chance to hold my peace,
  These stones to praise thee may not cease.
O let thy blessed *sacrifice* be mine,
And sanctify this *altar* to be thine.[18]
—George Herbert

God, You made sun and moon to distinguish seasons and day and night. And we cannot have the fruits of the earth but in their seasons. But You hath made no decree to distinguish the seasons of Your mercies. In Paradise the fruits were ripe the first minute, and in Heaven it is always autumn. Your mercies are ever in their maturity. You never say we should have come yesterday. You never say we must come back tomorrow, but today if we will hear your voice, You will hear us.

    You brought light out of darkness, not out of lesser light. You can bring Thy summer out of winter, though You have no

spring. All occasions invite Your mercies and all times are Your seasons.[19]

—John Donne (personalized)

O Absolute Sovereign of the world! Thou art Supreme Omnipotence, Sovereign Goodness, Wisdom itself! Thou art without beginning and without end. Thy works are limitless, Thy perfections infinite, and Thy intelligence is supreme! Thou art a fathomless abyss of marvels. O Beauty, containing all other beauty! O great God, Thou art Strength itself. Would that I possessed at this moment all the combined eloquence and wisdom of men! Then, in as far as it is possible here below, where knowledge is so limited, I could strive to make known one of Thy innumerable perfections. The contemplation of these reveals to some extent the nature of Him who is our Lord and our only Good.[20]

—Teresa of Avila

There are no accidents.
Nothing is wasted in Your love, O God.
The sticks, the stones,
the mundane events,
the color,
the light
all emotion, even pain . . .
nothing is wasted,
not even the waiting—
with its silence humming
like locusts in the still summer heat.
Your synthesis of all the ordinary
wells up within me,
empowering and equipping me
to become what I have not been.
I am your ongoing work
in matter and time,
a life struck whole
by the majesty of the Divine.

One touch of Your breath gives life,
while everything that comes
is a gift You bring
out of darkness into light
the fusion of all experience in time.
You create me from the raw bones up.
You create me from water and light and dry earth,
from the terra-firma of everyday life
into a thing of beauty—
into a God-sent life.[21]

　　　　　　　　　　　　　—Patricia Baxter

Lord, it is not life to live,
　　If Thy presence Thou deny;
Lord, if Thou Thy presence give,
　　'Tis no longer death to die.
Source and giver of repose,
Singly from Thy smile it flows;
Peace and happiness are Thine;
Mine they are, if Thou art mine.[22]
　　　　　　　—A. M. Toplady

Dear God,
I didn't think orange went with purple
until I saw the sunset
you made on Tue.
That was *cool*.[23]

　　　　　　　—Eugene (child)

To Jesus, the Crown of my Hope,
My soul is in haste to be gone;
Oh bear me, ye cherubims, up,
And waft me away to His throne.

My Savior, whom absent I love,
Whom not having seen I adore,

Whose Name is exalted above
All glory, dominion, and power.

Dissolve Thou the bond that detains
My soul from her portion in Thee,
And strike off the adamant chains
And make me eternally free.

When that happy era begins,
When arrayed in Thy beauty I shine,
Nor pierce anymore, by my sins,
The bosom on which I recline.

Oh then shall the veil be removed
And round me Thy brightness be poured.
I shall meet Him whom absent I loved;
I shall see whom unseen I adored.

And then never more shall the fears,
The trials, temptations, and woes,
Which darken this valley of tears,
Intrude on my blissful repose.

Or, if yet remembered above,
Remembrance no sadness shall raise;
They will be but new signs of Thy love,
New themes for my wonder and praise.

Thus the strokes which from sin and from pain
Shall set me eternally free
Will but strengthen and rivet the chain
Which binds me, my Savior, to Thee.[24]

—William Cowper

I do not know when I have had happier times in my soul, than when I have been sitting at work, with nothing before me but a candle and a white cloth, and hearing no sound but

that of my own breath, with You in my soul and heaven in my eye. . . . I rejoice in being exactly what I am—a creature capable of loving You and who, as long as I live, must be happy. I get up and look for a while out of the window and gaze at the moon and stars, the work of Your Almighty hand. I think of the grandeur of the universe and then sit down and think myself one of the happiest beings in it.[25]

—Anonymous Methodist woman,
eighteenth century (personalized)

All praise to Thee, my God, this night
for all the blessings of the light;
Keep me, O keep me, King of Kings,
beneath Thine own almighty wings.

Forgive me, Lord, for Thy dear Son,
the ill that I this day have done,
that with the world, myself, and Thee,
I, ere I sleep, at peace may be.

Teach me to live that I may dread
thy grace as little as my bed;
teach me to die that so I may
rise glorious at the judgment day.

O may my soul on Thee repose,
and with sweet sleep mine eyelids close;
Sleep that may me more vigorous make
to serve my God when I awake.

Praise God from whom all blessings flow;
praise Him all creatures here below;
praise Him above ye heavenly host
praise Father, Son, and Holy Ghost.[26]

—Thomas Ken

O Lord, our Lord,
how majestic is your name in all the earth!

You have set your glory
    above the heavens.
From the lips of children and infants
    you have ordained praise
because of your enemies,
    to silence the foe and avenger.

When I consider your heavens,
    the work of your fingers,
the moon and stars,
    which you have set in place,
what is man that you are mindful of him,
    the son of man that you care for him?
You made him a little lower than the heavenly beings
    and crowned him with glory and honor.

You made him ruler over the works of your hands;
    you put everything under his feet:
all flocks and herds,
    and the beasts of the field,
the birds of the air,
    and the fish of the sea,
    all that swim the paths of the seas.

—King David
Psalm 8 NIV

Now unto him that is able to do exceeding abundantly above
all that we ask or think, according to the power that worketh
in us, unto him be glory in the church by Christ Jesus throughout all ages, world without end.

—Paul, the apostle
Ephesians 3:20–21 KJV

3
Prayers of Surrender

Father, I want to know Thee, but my coward heart fears to give up its toys. I cannot part with them without inward bleeding, and I do not try to hide from Thee the terror of the parting. I come trembling, but I do come. Please root from my heart all those things which I have cherished so long and which have become a very part of my living self, so that Thou mayest enter and dwell there without a rival. Then shalt Thou make the place of Thy feet glorious. Then shall my heart have no need of the sun to shine in it, for Thyself wilt be the light of it. And there shall be no night there.[1]

—A. W. Tozer

Lord, we have taken a great fall,
and You have caught us in Your gentle, loving hands.
Lord, our tears have fallen like tiny waterfalls,
and You have dried them with Your love.
Lord, we needed someone to blame—and chose You.
This was wrong, but the way You replied
was by forgiving us and comforting us even more.
Lord, there is no way of telling You

how much Your love is helping us get through this tragedy, so we will only say this: "Thank You."[2]

—Abby

This Oklahoma fifth grader wrote this response following the 1995 bombing of the Murrah Federal Building in her city.

> O break my heart, but break it as a field
>   Is by the plough up-broken for the corn;
> O break it as the buds, by green leaf sealed
>   Are, to unloose the golden blossom torn.
> Love would I offer unto love's great Master,
>   Set free the odor, break the alabaster.
>
> O break my heart, break it victorious God,
>   That life's eternal well may flash abroad;
> O let it break as when the captive trees,
>   Breaking cold bonds, regain their liberties;
> And as thought's sacred grove to life is springing,
>   Be joys, like birds, their hope, Thy victory singing.[3]
>
> —Thomas Toke Bunch

Lord, we do not know what this life has in store for us, but be it good or bad, we are willing to be used by You. Use us until that moment comes when we go from service good to service best—when You begin to use us in glory.[4]

—Corrie ten Boom

Corrie wrote this prayer in a Nazi prison camp on a day when she believed she would be exterminated. A Dutch girl asked her, "How do you know all this that you have told me about Jesus?" Corrie told her that she got it from the Bible. The girl placed her faith in the Lord Jesus as they stood together that morning. Then, instead of being killed, Corrie was set free.

Lord, if any have to die this day,
let it be me,
for I am ready.[5]

—Billy Bray

Bray was converted from a life of drunken blasphemy. He allegedly said this prayer each morning as he waited to begin the day shift in the Cornwall tin mines.

God, give us grace to accept with serenity the things that cannot be changed, courage to change the things that should be changed, and the wisdom to distinguish the one from the other.[6]

—Christoph Friedrich
(pastor, 1782)

To have each day the thing I wish,
    Lord, that seems best to me;
But not to have the thing I wish,
    Lord, that seems best to Thee.
Most truly, then, Thy will be done,
    When mine, O Lord, is crossed;
'Tis good to see my plans o'erthrown,
    My ways in Thine all lost.[7]

—H. Bonar

In me there is darkness,
But with you there is light;
I am lonely, but you do not leave me;
I am feeble in heart, but with you there is help;
I am restless, but with you there is peace.
In me there is bitterness, but with you there is patience;
I do not understand your ways,
But you know the way for me.

Lord Jesus Christ,
You were poor and in distress,

A captive and forsaken as I am.
You know all man's troubles;
You abide with me
when all men fail me;
You remember and seek me;
It is your will that I should know you and turn to you.
Lord, I hear your call and follow;
Help me.[8]

—Dietrich Bonhoeffer

Bonhoeffer was imprisoned and martyred by Nazis in 1945.

I know the night is drawing near,
  The mists lie low on hill and bay,
The autumn sheaves are dewless, dry,
  But I have had the day.

Yes, I have had, dear Lord, the day,
  When at Thy call I have the night,
Brief be the twilight as I pass
  From light to dark, from dark to light.[9]

—Weir Mitchell

O great and unsearchable God, who knowest my heart, and triest all my ways; with a humble dependence upon the support of thy Holy Spirit, I yield myself up to thee, as thine own reasonable sacrifice, I return to thee thine own.[10]

—Charles H. Spurgeon

O merciful God,
Be Thou unto me a strong tower of defence
I humbly entreat Thee.
Give me grace to await Thy leisure
And patiently to bear what Thou doest unto me;
Nothing doubting or mistrusting Thy goodness towards me:
For Thou knowest what is good for me better than I do.
Therefore do with me in all things

what Thou wilt;
only arm me, I beseech Thee
with Thine armour that I may stand fast;
above all things, taking to me the shield of faith;
praying always that I may refer myself wholly to Thy will,
abiding Thy pleasure and comforting myself
in those troubles which it shall please Thee to send me,
seeing such troubles are profitable for me;
and I am assuredly persuaded that
all Thou doest cannot but be well.
And unto Thee be all honour and glory.[11]

> —Lady Jane Grey,
> during her final imprisonment

Lord, whose spirit is so good and so gentle in all things, and who art so compassionate that not only all prosperity but even all afflictions that come to Thine elect are the results of thy compassion. Grant me grace that I may not do as the pagans do in the condition to which thy justice has reduced me; grant that as a true Christian, I may recognize thee as my Father and as my God in whatever estate I find myself, since the change in my condition brings no change in thine own. . . . Grant then, Lord, that I may conform to thy will, just as I am, that being sick as I am, I may glorify thee in my sufferings.[12]

> —Blaise Pascal

This was Pascal's prayer when he learned his illness would lead to death.

> Take all, great God, I will not grieve,
> But still will wish that I had still to give;
>   I hear Thy voice, Thou bidd'st me quit
> My paradise; I bless and do submit;
>   I will not murmur at Thy word,
> Nor beg Thine angel to sheath up his sword.[13]

> —Anonymous,
> *Lincoln's Devotional*

God, I am traveling out to death's sea,
  I, who exulted in sunshine and laughter,
Dreamed not of dying—death is such a waste of me!
Grant me one prayer: Doom not the hereafter
Of mankind to war, as though I had died not—
  I, who in battle, my comrade's arm linking,
Shouted and sang, life in my pulses hot—
Throbbing and dancing! Let not my sinking
In dark be for naught, my death a vain thing;
God, let me know it, the end of man's fever!
Make my last breath a bugle call, carrying
Peace o'er the valleys and cold hills forever.[14]

             —John Galsworthy

Lord, open the King of England's eyes.[15]

             —William Tyndale

Tyndale uttered this prayer before he was burned at the stake by order of King Henry VIII for translating the Bible into English.

When my father died
I cried and cried
until I was weak.
After a while I couldn't cry anymore.
The tears wouldn't come.
Instead a strange hope
began to grow inside of me.
It was as if I were waking from a very long sleep
and everything around me had changed.

My father was still lying in the casket.
He seemed to be waiting for me
to stop feeling sorry for myself
and to discover what had happened to him.
Slowly, as I looked at him,
my father was my father again.

All the crooked laughter lines
around his eyes were as real as ever.

I realized then that
my father was living through death.
He was discovering the mystery of death
the way a child first discovers life.
He was enjoying the birth pangs of a new life.
His first life had been accepted and sealed with death.
He was passing through the world of death
where Christ is at work creating men for new tasks,
for new exciting worlds,
for new celebrations.

At that moment You said, Yes, God;
Yes to death and Yes to life.
The difference between life and death seemed to vanish.
My father was alive in death;
And You said Yes! to me that day.[16]
                                    —Debbie (adolescent)

O my Father, if it be possible, let this cup pass from me: never-theless, not as I will, but as Thou wilt.
                                    —Jesus Christ
                                    Matthew 26:39 KJV,
                                    prayed in Gethsemane

If, O Lord, you wish to make me a fresh spectacle before men and angels, may your holy will be done.[17]
                                    —Mme. Jeanne Guyon

Jealous church leaders imprisoned Mme. Guyon in the Bastille af-ter she traveled throughout France, teaching prayer and telling the people that Christianity was a matter of the heart.

Put out my eyes, and I can see You still;
slam my ears too, and I can hear You yet;
and without my feet can go to You;
and tongueless, I can conjure You at will.
Break off my arms, I shall take hold of You
and grasp You with my heart as with a hand;
arrest my heart, my brain will beat as true;
and if you set this brain of mine afire,
then on my bloodstream I will carry You.[18]

        —Rainer Maria Rilke

What are friends? What are comforts? What are sorrows? What are distresses? The time is short: It remains, that they which weep be as though they wept not, and they which rejoice as though they rejoiced not, for the fashion of this world passeth away. Oh, come, Lord Jesus, come quickly. Amen.[19]

        —David Brainerd

Brainerd was a missionary to the American Indians. He died at age 29.

Oh that the things which were seen and heard in this extraordinary person; his holiness, labour and self-denial in life; his heart and practice to the glory of God; and the wonderful frame of mind manifested in so steadfast a manner, under the expectation of death, and under the pains and agonies which brought it on; may excite in us all, both ministers and people, a due sense of the greatness of the work which we have to do in the world, of the excellency and amiableness of thorough religion in experience and practice, of the blessedness of the end of those whose death finishes such a life, and of the infinite value of their eternal reward . . . and effectually stir us up to constant endeavors that, in the way of such a holy life, we may at last come to as blessed an end! Amen.[20]

        —Jonathan Edwards

Edwards, David Brainerd's intended father-in-law, spoke this prayer at Brainerd's funeral.

> O God, Thou puttest into my heart this great desire to devote myself to the sick and sorrowful. I offer it to Thee.[21]
> —Florence Nightingale

Though her wealthy family protested vehemently, Florence gave her life to the sick and wounded. Ministering so lovingly and efficiently to the wounded during the Crimean War, she was appointed supervisor of all hospitals in her region.

4
Prayers of Thanksgiving

Lord God, how full our cup of happiness!
We drink and drink—and yet it grows not less;
But every morn the newly risen sun
Finds it replenished, sparkling, overrun.
Hast Thou not given us raiment, warmth, and meat,
And in due season all earth's fruits to eat?
Work for our hands and rainbows for our eyes,
And for our souls the wings of butterflies?
A father's smile, a mother's fond embrace,
The tender light upon a lover's face?
The talk of friends, the twinkling eye of mirth,
The whispering silence of the good green earth?
Hope for our youth and memories for age,
And psalms upon the heaven's moving page?
And dost Thou not of pain a mingling pour,
To make the cup but overflow the more?[1]

—Gilbert Thomas

O most merciful and gracious God, thou Fountain of all
mercy and blessing. Thou hast opened the hand of thy mercy
to fill me with blessings and the sweet effects of thy

lovingkindness. Thou feedest us like a Shepherd, thou lovest us as a friend and thinkest on us perpetually, as a careful mother on her helpless babe and art exceeding merciful to all that fear thee.

As thou hast spread thy hand upon me for a covering, so also enlarge my heart with thankfulness; and let thy gracious favors and lovingkindness endure forever and ever upon thy servant. Grant that what thou hast sown in mercy may spring up in duty; and let thy grace so strengthen my purposes that I may sin no more, but walk in the paths of thy commandments; that I, living here to the glory of thy name, may at last enter into the glory of my Lord, to spend a whole eternity in giving praise to thy ever glorious name.[2]

—Jeremy Taylor

Dear Lord, thank you that today, still seething and suffering from inner wounds, I found myself seated on a bus beside that small, shabby man. I realized, as he stared fixedly out the window, that he was struggling not to cry. My own little hurt seemed to shrink before the enormity of his. I knew I must speak to him—and did.

He turned to me, Lord, and drew from his threadbare wallet a picture of a bright-eyed little girl, six years old.

"We lost her yesterday," he said.

He was going now to pick out flowers. He wanted to talk about it. He was glad somebody cared. In our few blocks' ride across the city we shared it—his pride in her and his great loss.

We touched upon the mystery of being born at all, of being parents, of the brevity and beauty of life upon your earth. And when we parted he was actually smiling, "You've made me feel so much better," he said.

"You've made me feel better too," I told him. For my own petty pain no longer mattered. It was as if some balance had been struck between that which is hurtful and that which is healing.

Thank you that I have learned this lesson, Lord. Next time it surely won't be so hard to overcome an unexpected hurt.[3]
—Marjorie Holmes (excerpted)

Jesus Savior, gentle Shepherd
   Bless thy little lamb tonight.
In the darkness be thou near me
   Keep me safe 'till morning light.

All this day thy hand has led me
   And I thank thee for thy care.
Thou hast warmed me, clothed me, fed me.
   Listen to my evening prayer.[4]
—Don Moeller

Moeller began reciting this evening prayer as a child and continued to pray it into adulthood. A severe sinus infection took the sight in one eye and almost took his life, but Moeller continues faithfully serving God in ways that he can.

Thank you, Master Teacher,
for good role models;
for their inspiration
and tacit lessons
of strength and courage.
Thank you for words spoken
in wisdom and gentleness;
for parents and other teachers
who let me know
there is no nobler calling.
How blessed is the relationship
between teacher and student,
Lord, for in truth
both teacher and student
are both and the other:
This student is now a teacher,

but this teacher always will be a student.
Thank you for the call to teach and to learn.[5]
—Patricia Ann Meyers

Father, I thank you that you have heard me. I knew that you always hear me, but I said this for the benefit of the people standing here, that they may believe that you sent me.
—Jesus Christ
John 11:41–42 NIV

After Jesus uttered this prayer, He called out in a loud voice, "Lazarus, come out!" The dead man came out of the tomb, his hands and feet wrapped with strips of linen, and a cloth around his face.

Dear heavenly Father,

Thank you for determining my preappointed times and the boundaries of my dwellings, so that I would seek You out, in the hopes that I might long for You and find You. For in You I live and move and have my being.

Thank you, Lord Jesus, for leaving your heavenly home and coming into a sinful fallen world in order to save me from my sins and the just punishment which I deserve. Thank you for becoming familiar with my sufferings, that you might comfort me in my times of trial and affliction. Thank you for teaching me the true meaning of love, for you are God and God is love. Thank you for all your promises, especially for your promise to be with me always, even to the end of this age.

Thank you for teaching me how to pray, that I might have true fellowship with the Father, Son, and Holy Spirit. Thank you heavenly Father for all the temporal, physical, and spiritual provisions you have made for me here in my earthly journey. Thank you for choosing me to have such a visible affliction before others, that your strength may be made perfect through my weaknesses. Thank you for turning for me my mourning into laughter, and my desolation into joy; and for making my heart rejoice with joy unspeakable and full of glory.[6]
—Johnny Farese

John is a friend who suffers from muscular atrophy. His body is dwarfed and twisted, his arms and legs deformed and unusable. He cannot rise from bed; he can't even sit up. I was surprised by this prayer, composed on his voice-generated computer. John's prayer acknowledges his affliction, but it is mostly a psalm of thanksgiving to a God he loves deeply.

> I kneel not now to pray that Thou
>   Make white one single sin,
> I only kneel to thank Thee, Lord,
>   For what I have not been—
>
> For deeds which sprouted in my heart
>   But ne'er to bloom were brought,
> For monstrous vices which I slew
>   In the shambles of my thought—
>
> Dark seeds the world has never guessed,
>   By hell and passion bred,
> Which never grew beyond the bud
>   That cankered in my head.
>
> Some said I was a righteous man—
>   Poor fools! The gallows tree
> (If Thou hadst let one foot to slip)
>   Had grown a limb for me.[7]
>   —Harry Kemp

> O Lord, I ain't what I wants to be,
> O Lord, I ain't what I oughts to be,
> And, O Lord, I ain't what I'se gonna be,
> But, thank ya, Lord, I ain't what I used to be.[8]
>   —Prayer of an early slave

God of my forefathers, I cry unto Thee. Thou hast been the refuge of good and wise men in every generation. When history began, Thou wert the first enlightener of men's minds, and Thine was the Spirit that first led them out of their brutish estate and made them men. Through all the ages Thou hast been the Lord and giver of life, the source of all knowledge, the fountain of all goodness.

O Thou who wast, and art, and art to come, I thank Thee that this Christian way whereon I walk is no untried or uncharted road, but a road beaten hard by the footsteps of saints, apostles, prophets, and martyrs. I thank Thee for the finger posts and danger signals with which it is marked at every turning and which may be known to me through the study of the Bible, and of all history, and of all the great literature of the world. Beyond all, I give Thee devout and humble thanks for the great gift of Jesus Christ, the Pioneer of our faith. I praise Thee that Thou hast caused me to be born in an age and in a land which have known His name, and that I am not called upon to face any temptation or trial which He did not first endure.

Forbid it, Holy Lord, that I should fail to profit by these great memories of the ages that are gone by, or fail to enter into the glorious inheritance which Thou hast prepared for me, through Jesus Christ my Lord.[9]

—John Baille (excerpted)

God, You have been too good to me,
You don't know what You've done.
A clod's too small to drink in all
The treasure of the sun.

The pitcher fills the lifted cup
And still the blessings pour.
They overbrim the shallow rim
With cool refreshing store.

You are too prodigal with joy,
Too careless of its worth,
To let the stream with crystal gleam
Fall wasted on the earth.

Let many thirsty lips draw near
And quaff the greater part!
There still will be too much for me
To hold in one glad heart.[10]
                          —Charles Wharton Stork

My Lord, I made this song for you
To thank you for all that you've done for me.
I know I cannot repay you,
So, Lord, I thank you so much.

In times of pain and in suffering
I turn to you for your help.
You're always there to help me, Lord.
So, Lord, thank you so much.[11]
                          —Margaret Kaupuni

   Margaret sang this prayer song at a church in Hawaii after suffering forty-seven years of exile as a leper. Because of her leprosy, her four children were taken from her at birth and put up for adoption.

Lord, I have learned
Something of the meaning of grace.
To this man, mean and drab,
You gave the choicest of the choice;
To the undeserving You gave life,
And through her life I saw You
Lived out in sweetness—
Steadfast, enduring in virtue.
You gave me the best You had,
So with my hushed heart, bowed head
Accept my sacrifice of thanks.
Anne of the gentle brown eyes
Was Yours and mine.[12]
                          —Anthony Fortosis

This poem was written by my father after cancer claimed my mother's life.

Thanks be unto. Thee, O God, for every good and perfect gift from the treasury of heaven. We thank Thee for daily necessities, for without them we cannot live. But in a special way we thank Thee for the niceties of life: for music—those who compose and those who sing and play; for the painting of the artists; the writing of the poets and philosophers; the publishers of newspapers and magazines. We give Thee grateful praise for those who are dedicating their scientific talents for the improvement of life: the chemists, physicists, architects, and engineers—whose daily endeavors will be responsible for the new conveniences and beauties of tomorrow. For all these, and every other unremembered gift, we praise Thy holy name, and pray through Christ our Lord.[13]

—William Kadel

5

Prayers for Spiritual Growth

Lord, teach us to pray. Some of us are not skilled in the art of prayer. As we draw near to Thee in thought, our spirits long for Thy Spirit, and reach out for Thee, longing to feel Thee near. We know not how to express the deepest emotions that lie hidden in our hearts.

In these moments, we have no polished phrases with which to impress one another, no finely molded, delicately turned clauses to present to Thee. Nor would we be confined to weary petitions and repeat our prayers like the unwinding of a much-exposed film. We know, our Father, that we are praying most when we are saying least. We know that we are closest to Thee when we have left behind the things that have held us captive so long.

We would not be ignorant in prayer and, like children, only make want lists for Thee. Rather, we pray that Thou wilt give unto us only what we really need. We would not make our prayers the importuning of Thee, an omnipotent God, to do only what we want Thee to do. Rather, give us the vision, the courage, that shall enlarge our horizons and

stretch our faith to the adventure of seeking Thy loving will for our lives.

We thank Thee that Thou art hearing us even now. We thank Thee for the grace of prayer. We thank Thee for Thyself.[1]

—Peter Marshall

> Batter my heart, three-person'd God; for you
> As yet but knock, breathe, shine, and seek to mend;
> That I may rise and stand, o'erthrow me and bend
> Your force to break, blow, burn, and make me new.
> I, like an usurpt town, to another due,
> Labour to admit you, but oh, to no end,
> Reason your viceroy in me, me should defend,
> But is captiv'd, and proves weak or untrue.
> Yet dearly I love you, and would be loved faine,
> But am betroth'd unto your enemy:
> Divorce me, untie, or break that knot again,
> Take me to you, imprison me, for I
> Except you enthrall me, never shall be free,
> Nor ever chaste, except you ravish me.[2]

—John Donne

Dear God, help me in my weakness not to be afraid to live and to try my wings in directions which seem right for me and my family. On the other hand, keep me from using this freedom to rationalize and run away from responsibility when the present situation gets rough. Help me to realize today that I am free either to stay or go, knowing that You can take the failures and mistakes resulting from my bad decisions and some day possibly turn them into wisdom and sensitivity in relations with other people. Pray for me, Lord, I do not know how to pray about success and failure. So often I have been wrong in determining that which I thought would be best for me.[3]

—Keith Miller

Teach it again to us, O living God! Teach us to renew ourselves, O Jesus, who wept bitter tears in Gethsemane. Help us to forget the long way of pain and strife through which we've come, each of us dragging a cross to some Calvary in our hearts. Help us to forget the hours of utter darkness when we have lost the way. Help us to forget our hates, fears and the bitter thoughts that divide us.

Help us to remember the upclimbing will that is a staff unto our feet. Nourish in us every tiny impulse to help each other. Give us more love, more compassion, more sincerity one to another.

Help us to appreciate the present moment and to search out its advantages that we may be glad for the todays of life, leaving the tomorrows in Thy hand. Steady us to do our full stint of work. Help us to rise each day with new sympathies, new thoughts of unity and joy.[4]

—Helen Keller

Dear God,
why do I keep fighting you off?
One part of me wants you desperately,
another part of me unknowingly
pushes you back and runs away.
What is there in me that
so contradicts my desire for you?
These transition days, these passageways
are calling me to let go of old securities,
to give myself over into your hands.

Like Jesus who struggled with the pain
I, too, fight the "let it all be done."
Loneliness, lostness, non-belonging—
all these hurts strike out at me,
leaving me pained with this present goodbye.
I want to be more but I fight the growing.
I want to be new but I hang onto the old.
I want to live but I won't face the dying.

I want to be whole but I cannot bear
to gather up the pieces into one.

Is it that I refuse to be out of control,
to let the tears take their humbling journey,
to allow my spirit to feel its depression,
to stay with the insecurity of "no home"?
Now is the time. You call to me,
begging me to let you have my life,
inviting me to taste the darkness,
so I can be filled with the light,
allowing me to lose my direction
so that I will find my way home to you.[5]

—Joyce Rupp

Deliver me, O God, from the enemies of my soul.
I am no longer afraid of men who stand in my way,
    even of those who
obstruct your purposes and deceive their fellowmen
    with their arrogant and clever cliches.
They anger me, but they do not frighten me.
My pain and confusion come by way of my own weak-
    nesses and faithlessness.
I strive for success and am fractured by failure.
I reach for ecstasy and am clobbered with depression.
I wait for guidance and Your heavens are gray with
    silence.
I ask for infilling and am confronted with emptiness.
I seek opportunities and run into stone walls.
I overcome these pernicious demons in the morning—
    only to face them again when day turns to night.
They refuse to die, these persistent devils.
They plague my days and haunt my nights and rob me
    of the peace and joy of God-motivated living.
And yet, O Lord, you have surrounded my life like a
    great fortress.

There is nothing that can touch me save by your loving permission.[6]

—Leslie Brandt
(inspired by Psalm 59)

Lord, make my soul
To mirror Thee,
Thyself alone
To shine in me,
That men may see
Thy love, Thy grace,
Nor note the glass
That shows Thy face.[7]
—Blanche Mary Kelly

Search me, O God search me and know my heart,
Try me and prove me in the hidden part;
Cleanse me and make me holy as Thou art,
And lead me in the way everlasting.

Give me the heart that naught can change or chill,
The love that loves unchanged through good or ill,
The joy that through all trials triumphs still,
And lead me in the way everlasting.

Take my poor heart and only let me love
The things that always shall abiding prove;
Bind all my heart-strings to the world above,
And lead me in the way everlasting.[8]
—A. B. Simpson

Dear Lord, make us tolerant of those whose opinions differ from our own. Help us to be charitable and kind, forgiving and understanding. Where men are overbearing and unreasonable, grant that we may be patient and trustful. Free us from the reputation of being opinionated. Where life is hardened by our negligence, make it solvent by Thy Spirit's guidance. Make us

useful in Thy redemptive purpose, so that Thy kingdom may come into the lives of others also. Amen.[9]

—John L. Sandlin

O Lord of the Oceans,
My little bark sails on a restless sea,
Grant that Jesus may sit at the helm and steer me safely;
Suffer no adverse currents to divert my heavenward course;
Let not my faith be wrecked amid storms and shoals.
Bring me to harbor with flying pennants, hull unbreached,
    cargo unspoiled.
I ask great things, expect great things, shall receive great things;
I venture on thee wholly, fully—my wind, sunshine, anchor,
    defense. . . .
The voyage is long, the waves high, the storms pitiless,
But my helm is held steady, thy Word secures safe passage,
Thy grace wafts me onward, my haven is guaranteed.
This day will bring me nearer home;
Grant me holy consistency in every transaction,
        my peace flowing as a running tide,
        my righteousness as every chasing wave.
Help me to live circumspectly, with skill to convert every care
    into prayer,
Halo my path with gentleness and love,
        smooth every asperity of temper,
        let me not forget how easy it is to occasion grief,
        may I strive to bind up every wound,
        and pour oil on all troubled waters.
May the world this day be happier and better because I live.
Let my mast before me be the Savior's cross,
And every oncoming wave the fountain in his side.
Help me, protect me in the moving sea
        until I reach the shore of unceasing praise.[10]

—Puritan Prayer

O Lord, how many of us would be more concerned about our character if we realized that by our unconscious influence we

are impressing other lives for good or ill. It is a sobering thought
that what I say or do touches the deepest part of others' lives,
and even the atmosphere I carry with me betokens the inner
reality of my own life. Help me to stand in awe of this spiritual energy, so silent and invisible and yet so powerful. May I
realize that there is something subtle and magnetic emanat-
ing from me, and that its impact upon others will be either
helpful or hurtful, whether I will it or not. May I employ this
way to help society fundamentally and lastingly by the silent,
powerful contagion of a thoroughly good life.

And in relation to my talents, too often I sulk in idleness
because I imagine my capacities are limited when I have never
put them to the test. I say, if I knew more, if I had more money,
if my environment was different, if my health was better, if my
personality was more magnetic—I could do wonders for you.
But the gifts I already have, touched by Thy Spirit, could accom-
plish great results. Teach me that the path of present faithful-
ness is the only path leading to larger service in the future.

In the name of Him whose very garments conveyed healing
and holy helpfulness.[11]

—Frederick Lewis

It's sundown, Lord.
The shadows of my life stretch back
    into the dimness of the years long spent.
I fear not death, for that grim foe betrays himself at last,
    thrusting me forever into life:
Life with you, unsoiled and free.
But I do fear.
I fear the Dark Spectre may come too soon—
    or do I mean, too late?
That I should end before I finish or
    finish, but not well.
That I should stain your honor, shame your name,
    grieve your loving heart.
Few, they tell me, finish well. . . .
Lord, let me get home before dark.

The darkness of a spirit
   grown mean and small, fruit shriveled on the vine,
   bitter to the taste of my companions,
   burden to be borne by those brave few who
   love me still.
No, Lord. Let the fruit grow lush and sweet,
   A joy to all who taste;
Spirit-sign of God at work,
   stronger, fuller, brighter at the end.
Lord, let me get home before dark.

The darkness of tattered gifts,
   rust-locked, half-spent or ill-spent,
A life that once was used of God
   now set aside.
Grief for glories gone or
Fretting for a task You never gave.
Mourning in the hollow chambers of memory,
Gazing on the faded banners of victories long gone.
Cannot I run well unto the end?
Lord, let me get home before dark.

The outer me decays—
   I do not fret or ask reprieve.
The ebbing strength but weans from mother earth
   and grows me up for heaven.
I do not cling to shadows cast by immortality.
I do not patch the scaffold lent to build the real, eternal me.
I do not clutch about me my cocoon,
   vainly struggling to hold hostage
   a free spirit pressing to be born.

But will I reach the gate
   in lingering pain, body distorted, grotesque?
Or will it be a mind
   wandering untethered among light
            phantasies or grim terrors?

Of your grace, Father, I humbly ask. . . .
Let me get home before dark.[12]
—Robertson McQuilkin

Blessed Creator,
Thou hast promised thy beloved sleep;
Give me restoring rest needful for tomorrow's toil.
If dreams be mine, let them not be tinged with evil.
Let thy Spirit make my time of repose a blessed
temple of his holy presence.
May my frequent lying down make me familiar with
  death,
      the bed I approach remind me of the grave,
        the eyes I now close picture to me their final
          closing.
Keep me always ready, waiting for admittance to thy
  presence.
Weaken my attachment to earthly things.
May I hold life loosely in my hand,
      knowing that I receive it on condition of its
        surrender;
As pain and suffering betoken transitory health,
      may I not shrink from a death
      that introduces me to the freshness of eternal
        youth.
I retire this night in full assurance of one day awaking
  with thee.
All glory for this precious hope,
      for the gospel of grace,
      for thine unspeakable gift of Jesus,
      for the fellowship of the Trinity.
Withhold not thy mercies in the night season;
      thy hand never wearies
      thy power needs no repose,
      thine eye never sleeps.
Help me when I helpless lie,
      when my conscience accuses me of sin,

when my mind is harassed by foreboding thoughts,
when my eyes are held awake by personal anxieties.
Show thyself to me as the God of all grace, love, and power;
  thou hast a balm for every wound,
    a solace for all anguish,
    a remedy for every pain,
    a peace for all disquietude.
Permit me to commit myself to thee awake or asleep.[13]

—Puritan Prayer

God, let me be aware.
Let me not stumble blindly down the ways,
Just getting somehow safely through the days,
Not even groping for another hand,
Not even wondering why it all was planned;
Eyes to the ground unseeking for the light,
Soul never aching for a wild-winged flight.
Please, keep me eager just to do my share.

God, let me be aware.
God—let me be aware.
Stab my soul fiercely with others' pain,
Let me walk seeing horror and stain.
Let my hands, groping, find other hands.
Give me the heart that divines, understands.
Give me the courage, wounded, to fight.
Flood me with knowledge, drench me in light.
Please—keep me eager just to do my share.
God—let me be aware.[14]

—Miriam Teichner

Teach us good Lord, to serve Thee as Thou deservest:
To give and not count the cost;
To fight and not heed the wounds;
To toil and not to seek for rest;
To labor and not ask for reward—
Save that of knowing that we do Thy will.[15]

—Ignatius of Loyola

O dear Savior, be not impatient with us—educate us for a higher life, and let that life begin here. May we be always in the school, always disciples, and when we are out in the world may we be trying to put into practice what we have learned at Jesus' feet. What he tells us in darkness may we proclaim in the light, and what he whispers in our ear in the closets may we sound forth upon the housetops.[16]

—Charles H. Spurgeon

I have no wit, no words, no tears;
   My heart within me like a stone
Is numbed too much for hopes or fears.
   Look right, look left, I dwell alone;
I lift my eyes, but dimmed with grief
   No everlasting hills I see;

My life is in the falling leaf:
   O Jesus quicken me.
My life is like a faded leaf,
   My harvest dwindled to a husk:
Truly my life is void and brief
   And tedious in the barren dusk;
My life is like a frozen thing,
   No bud or greenness can I see;
Yet rise it shall—the sap of Spring;
   O Jesus rise in me.

My life is like a broken bowl,
   A broken bowl that cannot hold
One drop of water for my soul
   Or cordial in the searching cold;
Cast in the fire the perished thing;
   Melt and remold it, till it be
A royal cup for Him, my King:
   O Jesus drink of me.[17]

—Christina Rossetti

I am only a spark
Make me a fire.
I am only a string
Make me a lyre.
I am only a drop
Make me a fountain.
I am only an ant hill
Make me a mountain.
I am only a feather
Make me a wing.
I am only a rag
Make me a king![18]
   —A prayer from Mexico

I do not ask for any crown
   But that which all may win;
Nor try to conquer any world
   Except the one within.
Be Thou my guide until I find
   Led by a tender hand,
The happy kingdom in myself
   And dare to take command.[19]
      —Louisa May Alcott

We must praise your goodness that you have left nothing undone to draw us to yourself. But one thing we ask of you, our
God, not to cease to work in our improvement. Let us tend
towards you, no matter by what means and be fruitful in good
works, for the sake of Jesus Christ our Lord.[20]
      —Ludwig van Beethoven

O Thou that hearest prayer,
Teach me to pray.
I confess that in religious exercises
the language of my lips and the feelings of my heart
  have not always agreed,

that I have frequently taken carelessly upon my tongue
a name never pronounced above without reverence and
  humility,
that I have often desired things which would have
  injured me,
that I have depreciated some of my chief mercies,
that I have erred both on the side of my hopes and also
  of my fears,
that I am unfit to choose for myself,
  for it is not in me to direct my steps.
Let thy Spirit help my infirmities for I know not what to pray
 as I ought.
Let him produce in me wise desires by which I may ask right
 things,
  then I shall know thou hearest me.
May I never be importunate for temporal blessings
    but always refer them to thy fatherly goodness,
    for thou knowest what I need before I ask;
May I never think I prosper unless my soul prospers,
    or that I am rich unless rich toward thee,
    or that I am wise unless wise unto salvation.
May I seek first thy kingdom and its righteousness.
May I value things in relation to eternity.
May my spiritual welfare be my chief solicitude.
May I be poor, afflicted, despised, and have thy blessing,
    rather than be successful in enterprise,
    or have more than my heart can wish,
    or be admired by my fellow-men,
    if thereby these things make me forget thee.
May I regard the world as dreams, lies, vanities, vexation of
 spirit,
    and desire to depart from it.
And may I seek my happiness in thy favor, image, presence,
 service.[21]

                          —Puritan Prayer

O Lord, reassure me with your quickening Spirit; without you I can do nothing. Mortify in me all ambition, vanity, vainglory, worldliness, pride, selfishness, and resistance from God, and fill me with love, peace, and all the fruits of the Spirit. O Lord, I know not what I am, but to you I flee for refuge. I would surrender myself to you, trusting your precious promises and against hope believing in hope. You are the same yesterday, today, and forever; and therefore, waiting on the Lord, I trust I shall at length renew my strength.[22]

—William Wilberforce

Wilberforce fought in England for the abolition of slavery.

O Lord, drench me with humility.[23]

—Oswald Chambers

As a timid teenager, Chambers often had only enough courage to say the prayer above at weekly prayer meetings in Rye Chapel, London.

O God, who hast commanded us to remember thee in the days of our youth, and dost promise that those who seek thee early shall find thee; make our vision bright, our allegiance unfaltering, our service loyal—through him who, even as a boy, was always about his Father's business, Jesus Christ thy Son, our Lord.[24]

—John R. Stott

Thou knowest, O Lord, that as I labor each day for my daily bread, working in the same office or at the same trade or repeating the same household tasks, I feel the deadening influence of routine. My finest faculties sicken and weaken under the process which involves a monotonous task. Show me how to escape the danger of dulled hopes, blunted sensibilities, and commonplace thinking. In my better moments I know that all things are possible with you and that Jesus is able to make all grace abound toward me. . . .

Clouds of mystery sometimes hide my origin and a veil is over my future. At times the desert plod makes life seem but a weary waste. Preserve me from the perils of my lot. Keep wonder and reverence alive. Help me not to become used to sin or deceived by glamor. Keep me steadfast despite the pettiness of men, the fret of care, the cruel toil, and the misunderstandings and strife.

May every human task be glorified and every human contact be freshened by the love and peace and vision which only You can bestow.[25]

—Frederick Lewis (excerpted)

O Jesus, Son of God, carpenter of Nazareth, grant sight to those blinded by luxury and deliverance to those bound by want, that the rich may joyfully follow the simplicity of thy most holy life, and the poor may obtain their inheritance, and that the hearts of all may be set with one accord to discover the way of salvation, through thy mercy who for our sake didst become poor that we, through thy poverty, might become rich. And this we ask for thy Name's sake.[26]

—Unknown author

I praise Thee, O God, for illuminating my mind and for enabling me to prove demonstratively that Thy wisdom is as infinite as Thy power. Help me to use these discoveries to praise and love and obey, and may I be exceedingly careful that my affections keep pace with my knowledge.

May I adore the mystery I cannot comprehend. Help me to be not too curious in prying into those secret things that are known only to Thee, O God—not too rash in censuring what I do not understand. May I not perplex myself about those methods of providence that seem to me involved and intricate, but resolve them into Thine infinite wisdom, who knowest the spirit of all flesh and dost best understand how to govern those souls Thou hast created.

We are of yesterday and know nothing. But Thy boundless mind comprehends, at one view, all things, past, present and

future, and as Thou dost see all things, Thou dost best understand what is good and proper for each individual and for me, with relation to both worlds. So deal with me, O my God.[27]

—Susanna Wesley

Wesley was the mother of nineteen children, including John and Charles Wesley.

Lord! Who thy thousand years dost wait
To work the thousandth part
Of Thy vast plan, for us create
With zeal a patient heart.[28]

—J. H. Newman

Across the Kidron valley
a grove of ancient olive trees
so dense a man could hide himself
until the storm had passed.

Entwined among the branches
an echo from another time,
an offer welcomed first by Eve
to choose a better way.

You weighed the matter, Jesus,
this finely reasoned argument
against a more exacting course,
and chose your Father's will.

When I would fix on comfort
in place of witness to my faith,
remind me of those gardens, Lord,
and what emerged from each.

From one fled pride far-fallen,
fond hopes, it seemed, forever dashed;

the other poured forth trust-made-flesh
to heal a wounded world.[29]
                                        —Roger Swenson

But O my God, though grovelling I appear
Upon the ground, and have a rooting here
Which pulls me downward, yet in my desire
To that which is above me I aspire;
But all my best affections I profess
To Him that is the Sun of Righteousness.
Oh! keep the morning of His incarnation,
The burning noontide of His bitter passion,
The night of His descending, and the height
Of His ascension—ever in my sight.
That, imitating Him in what I may,
I never follow an inferior way.[30]
                                        —George Wither

Blessed Master, with my whole heart I thank you for the wonderful lesson that the path to a life of answers to prayer is through the will of God. Lord, teach me to know this blessed will by living it, loving it, and always doing it. So shall I learn to offer prayers according to that plan, and to find in harmony with your blessed will my boldness in prayer and my confidence in accepting the answer.

Father, it is your will that your child should enjoy your presence and blessing. It is your will that everything in the life of your child should be in accordance with your desires, and that the Holy Spirit should work this in me. It is your will that your child should live in the daily experience of distinct answers to prayer, so as to enjoy living in direct fellowship with you. It is your plan that your name should be glorified in and through your children, and that it *shall* be in those who trust you. Father, let your will be my confidence in all I ask.

Blessed Savior, teach me to believe in the glory of your will—that holy desire, the eternal love which with divine power works out its purpose in each human will that yields itself to it. Lord,

teach me this. You can make me see how every promise and every command of the Word is indeed the will of God, and that its fulfillment is sure for me because my Father himself guarantees it. Let the will of God become to me the rock on which my prayer and my assurance of an answer ever rest.[31]

—Andrew Murray

God of the gallant trees,
Give to us fortitude;
Give as thou givest to these,
Valorous hardihood.
We are the trees of thy planting, O God;
We are the trees of thy wood.

Now let the life-sap run
Clean through our every vein.
Perfect what thou hast begun,
God of the sun and rain,
Thou who dost measure the weight of the wind,
Fit us for stress and for strain.[32]

—Amy Carmichael

O eternal God, though Thou art not such as I can see with my eyes or touch with my hands, yet grant me this day a clear conviction of Thy reality and power. Let me not go forth to my work believing only in the world of sense and time, but give me grace to understand that the world I cannot see or touch is the most real world of all. My life today will be lived in time, but eternal issues will be concerned in it. The needs of my body will claim attention, but it is for the needs of my soul that I must care most. My business will be with things material, but behind them let me be aware of things spiritual.

O God, who dwellest in light unapproachable, yet also lives within me, give me grace today to recognize the stirrings of Thy Spirit within my soul and to listen most attentively to all that Thou hast to say to me. Let not the noises of the world ever so confuse me that I cannot hear Thee speak, and suffer me never to deceive myself as to the meaning of Thy commands.

I thank Thee, O Lord, that thou hast so set eternity within my heart that no earthly thing can ever satisfy me wholly. I thank Thee that every present joy is so mixed with sadness and unrest as to lead my mind upwards to the contemplation of a more perfect blessedness. And above all I thank thee for the sure hope and promise of an endless life which thou hast given me in the glorious gospel of Jesus Christ my Lord.[33]

—John Baille

Dear Bread of Life, I confess that sometimes I feel so inadequate to meet the crowd of needs that surrounds me. Like that little boy with the lunch basket, I feel that the loaves I have are so small and the fish, so few. How far will they go among so many?

And yet I know that you manifest power through the weak things of the world. You used a barren couple past the age of childbearing to create a nation as populous as the sand on the seashore. You used a young shepherd with a slingshot to slay a giant. You used a poor little boy with five flat loaves of coarsely-ground barley bread and a couple of small fish to feed thousands.

Help me to see, Lord, that this is how you characteristically work. Help me to see that I don't need the adequate bank account Philip recommended or the abundant assets Andrew hinted at. All I need is to place what I have in your hands, like that little boy did.

Give me the faith to realize that you will bless what I give, no matter how small the loaves or how few the fish. No matter how meager the time or the talents or the treasures I place in your hands, you will multiply them.

I don't have much, Lord, but I give you what I have. Take my coarsely-ground life and the small skills that accompany it. Take them into your hands, Lord. Bless them. Multiply them. Use them for your glory and for the good of others.[34]

—Ken Gire

I'm hungry for something, Lord.
I have so much rich food and cake and candy for myself,
     but I'm hungry.
People around me seem so stiff and tight and hard to
     reach,
and they make me that way.
But I'm hungry for something more.
People I know keep talking about great ideas, brilliant
     questions,
and the problem of Your existence.
But I'm hungry for You, not ideas or theories.
I want You to touch me, to reach inside me and turn me
     on.
There are so many people who will counsel me to death,
But I am hungry for someone who really knows You and
     has You—
Someone who can get so close to me that I can see You
     there.
I have so many things, but I'm hungry for You.
Deep, deep down inside I'm hungry, even if I appear
to be silly, lazy, or unconcerned at times.
I'm hungry for Your kind of power and love and joy.
Feed me, Lord, feed me with Your rich food.[35]

                                 —Anonymous (adapted)

   Lord, make me an instrument of Your peace.
   Where there is hatred, let me sow love;
   Where there is injury, pardon;
   Where there is doubt, faith;
   Where there is despair, hope;
   Where there is darkness, light;
   And where there is sadness, joy.
   O, Divine Master, grant that I may not so much seek
   to be consoled as to console;
   To be understood as to understand;
   For it is in giving that we receive;

It is in pardoning that we are pardoned;
It is in dying that we are born to eternal life.[36]
—Francis of Assisi

O Master, let me rest my bones
against that wind-struck terebinth
beyond the grasp of your stern gaze.
The haste in your ascendant step
has weakened my naive resolve
to conquer Tabor's rocky slope.

You know, my Jesus, I began
with hopes of glory from on high,
but now amid the raging storm
I must repose and steel my nerves
against the searching lightning bolts
unleashed to seal and ratify.

The clouded peak awaits not me,
a fisherman unused to heights.
The urgent thunder calls for You;
upon your head whirls heaven's dove.
Go up, go up and let me dream
of bursting nets and wave-lapped shores.

And yet I know there waits above
a higher truth, a saving word;
so lift me, Master, from my fears,
that having come this far with you,
I may forsake the valley's charm
and know the upland's awful grace.[37]
—Roger Swenson

O Thou, "Crystal Christ, good Paragon of God," help me to see
how human, how simple and unaffected Thy goodness was:
forgiving an evil woman, lifting the children in Thine arms,
preparing breakfast for Thy friends, curing lepers, showing

disappointed fishermen how to make a catch. There was no pretense about Thy goodness. We would that all of us could be like Thee.

Alas for so much honesty that is only prudence, for so much chastity that dares not be otherwise, for so many good deeds that expect a return, for so much fidelity to the truth only for fear of being caught. Help me to gain that goodness which is genuine. Lure me by Thy example. Rule me by Thy Spirit. May I experience outbursts of real generosity, moral brakes that are automatic, ventures in Christian service that lead me along upper levels with the light of heaven on my path.[38]

—Frederick Lewis

God, though this life is but a wraith,
  Although we know not what we use,
Although we grope with little faith,
  Give me the heart to fight—and lose.

Ever insurgent let me be,
  Make me more daring than devout;
From sleek contentment keep me free,
  And fill me with a buoyant doubt.

Open my eyes to visions girt
  With beauty, and with wonder lit—
But let me always see the dirt,
  And all that spawn and die in it.

Open my ears to music, let
  Me thrill with Spring's first flutes and drums—
But never let me dare forget
  The bitter ballads of the slums.

From compromise and things half-done,
  Keep me, with stern and stubborn pride.
And when, at last the fight is won,
  God, keep me still unsatisfied.[39]

—Louis Untermeyer

Forbid it, Lord, that our roots become too firmly attached to this earth, that we should fall in love with things. Help us to understand that the pilgrimage of this life is but an introduction, a preface, a training school for what is to come. Then we see all of life in its true perspective. Then shall we not fall in love with the things of time, but come to love the things that endure. Then shall we be saved from the tyranny of possessions which we have no leisure to enjoy, of property whose care becomes a burden. Give us, we pray, the courage to simplify our lives.

So may we be mature in our faith, childlike but never childish, humble but never cringing, understanding but never conceited. So help us, O God, to live and not merely to exist, that we may have joy in our work. In thy name, who alone can give us moderation and balance and zest for living, we pray. Amen.[40]

—Peter Marshall

> The tumult and the shouting dies;
> The captains and the kings depart.
> Still stands Thine ancient sacrifice:
> An humble and a contrite heart.
> Lord God of Hosts,
> Be with us yet, lest we forget,
> Lest we forget.[41]
>
> —Rudyard Kipling

Almighty and everlasting God, who, by thy Holy Spirit,
didst preside in the Council of the blessed Apostles,
. . . save us from all error, ignorance, pride, and prejudice;
and of thy great mercy vouchsafe, we beseech thee,
so to direct, sanctify and govern us in our work,
by the mighty power of the Holy Ghost,
that the comfortable Gospel of Christ may be truly preached,
truly received, and truly followed in all places
to the breaking down of the kingdom of sin, Satan, and death;
till at length the whole of thy dispersed sheep,
being gathered into thy fold

shall become partakers of everlasting life,
through the merits and death of Jesus Christ our Savior. Amen.[42]
—*The Book of Common Prayer*

Lord, who createdst man in wealth and store,
Though foolishly he lost the same
Decaying more and more,
Till he became
Most poor:
With Thee
O let me rise
As larks, harmoniously,
And sing this day Thy victories:
Then shall the fall further the flight in me.

My tender age in sorrow did begin;
And still with sicknesses and shame
Thou didst so punish sin,
That I became
Most thin.
With Thee
And feel this day Thy victory;
For, if I imp my wing on Thine,
Affliction shall advance the flight in me.[43]
—George Herbert

Eternal Father,
It is amazing love
   that thou hast sent thy Son to suffer in my stead,
   that thou hast added the Spirit to teach, comfort, and guide,
   that thou hast allowed the ministry of angels to wall me round;
All heaven subserves the welfare of a poor worm.
Permit thy unseen servants to be ever active on my behalf,
   and to rejoice when grace expands in me.
Suffer them never to rest until my conflict is over,
   and I stand victorious on salvation's shore.

Grant that my proneness to evil, deadness to good,
   resistance to thy Spirit's motions,
   may never provoke thee to abandon me.
May my hard heart awake thy pity, not thy wrath,
And if the enemy gets an advantage through my corruption,
   let it be seen that heaven is mightier than hell,
   that those for me are greater than those against me.
Arise to my help in richness of covenant blessings,
Keep me feeding in the pastures of thy strengthening Word,
   searching Scripture to find thee there.
If my waywardness is visited with a scourge,
   enable me to receive correction meekly,
   to bless the reproving hand,
   to discern the motive for rebuke,
   to respond promptly, and do the first work.
Let all thy fatherly dealings make me a partaker of thy holiness.
Grant that in every fall I may sink lower on my knees,
And that when I rise it may be to loftier heights of devotion.
May my every cross be sanctified,
   every loss be gain,
   every denial a spiritual advantage,
   every dark day a light of the Holy Spirit,
   every night of trial of song.[44]
—Puritan Prayer

Lord, give me faith—to leave it all to Thee,
The future is Thy gift, I would not lift
The veil Thy love has hung 'twixt it and me.[45]
—John Oxenham

Five billion plus and counting, Lord,
the facets of your love
spread all around this clouded globe
so perfect from above.
A closer look reveals the faults,
the fissures caused by pride,
the yellow tinge of cowardice,

the stains of sin inside.
Yet you, dear Father, see it all,
the surface and the core,
beholding diamonds in the rough
on which you gently pour
the sacrificial, cleansing blood
that fell from Jesus' cross
to make of this unheeding race
a diadem from dross.
O, send your Holy Spirit now
with hope to clear our sight
that we may see this jeweled earth
reflected in your light.[46]
             —Roger Swenson

Lord, I believe; help thou mine unbelief.
             —Father of epileptic boy
             Mark 9:24 KJV

When this father made his plea, Jesus answered that all things are possible to those who believe.

Blessed Savior, with my whole heart I bless you for the appointment of the inner room as the school where you meet each of your pupils alone and reveal to each the Father. My Lord, strengthen my faith in the Father's tender love and kindness, so that my first instinctive thought when sinful or troubled may be to go where I know the Father awaits me and where prayer never can go unblessed. Let the thought that He knows my need before I ask bring me in great restfulness of faith, to trust that He will give what His child requires. Let the place of secret prayer become to me the most beloved spot of earth.

Lord, hear me as I pray that you would everywhere bless the closets of your believing people. Let your wonderful revelation of a Father's tenderness free all Christians from every thought of secret prayer as a duty or a burden and lead them to regard it as the highest privilege of their life, a joy and a blessing. Bring back all who are discouraged because they cannot find anything to bring to you in prayer. May they see they only need to come with their emptiness to you who has all to give—and delights to do it. Let their one thought be not what they have to bring the Father, but what the Father waits to give them.

Bless especially the inner room of all your servants as the place where your truth and grace are revealed to them, where they are daily anointed with fresh oil, where their strength is renewed, and the blessings with which they are to bless their fellowmen are received in faith. Lord, draw us all in the closet nearer to yourself and the Father.[47]

—Andrew Murray

Give me courage Lord
to take risks
not the usual ones
respected
necessary
relatively safe
but those I could avoid—
the go-for-broke ones.
I need courage
not just because
I may fall on my face or worse
but others seeing me
a sorry spectacle
if it should happen
will say
"he didn't know what he was doing"
or "he's foolhardy"
or "he's old enough to know
one leads from the side
instead of letting oneself be caught
in a wild stampede."
Give me courage Lord

to take unnecessary risks
to live at tension
instead of opting out.
Give me the guts to put up
instead of shutting up.[48]

—Joseph Bayly

6

Prayers of Questioning

Dear God, My mom and dad are divorced. For three years. Nobody's perfect. But why did you have to pick on us? I wish we were all with each other. Maybe you could have them get along on weekends.[1]

Please,
Stephen [age 11]

No one pays attention to me or what I say, Lord. . . . I tried to build a boat once but it fell apart. I tried to make the baseball team but I always threw past third base. I wrote some articles for our school paper but they didn't want them. I even tried out for the school play but the other kids laughed when I read my lines. . . .

I don't try anymore because I'm afraid to mess up. If only there was something I could do. . . . Something I could make that was my work, only mine. . . .

Lord, the world seems full of heroes and idols and important people.

Where are all the failures? Where are they hiding? Where are people like me? Did you ever fail, Lord? Do you know what it's like when everyone looks up at you and says, "He's a failure."[2]

—David (adolescent)

Dear God, Does Pat Robertson really know you personally? If not, I thought you'd like to know that he talks about you a lot.[3]

Your Friend,
Brent [age 8]

> Does it please you to oppress me,
>   to spurn the work of your hands,
>   while you smile on the schemes of the wicked?
> Do you have eyes of flesh?
> Do you see as a mortal sees?
> Are your days like those of a mortal
>   or your years like those of a man,
>   that you must search out my faults
>   and probe after my sin—
>   though you know that I am not guilty
>   and that no one can rescue me from your hand?
> Your hands shaped and made me.
> Will you turn now and destroy me?

—Job
Job 10:3–8 NIV

Dear God,

Why couldn't anyone in Israel get along in the Bible? There was always stone throwing and fighting. Jake, Joseph, Abe, Moses—you name them—no person was the friend of another. That's no good.[4]

—Roy [age 10]

Lord, what is man? Why should he cost thee
  So dear? What had his ruin lost thee?
Lord, what is man that thou hast overbought
  So much a thing of naught.

What is my faithless soul that I
  Would needs fall in
  With guilt and sin?
What did the Lamb, that he should die?
What did the Lamb, that he should need,
When the wolf sins, himself to bleed?

Why should his unstain'd breast make good
  My blushes with his own heart-blood?
O my Savior, make me see
  How dearly thou hast paid for me.
That lost again my life may prove
  As then in death, so now in love.[5]
               —Richard Crashaw

Dear God,
Instead of letting people die and having
to make new ones why don't you
just keep the ones you got now?[6]
               —Jane

Good morning, Jesus.
Time for me to get up
and get ready for school.
On second thought,
maybe I'll be sick instead.
I didn't finish my homework—
I still have three history chapters to read.
  I can't go.
I think I'm coming down with something.
Lord, how am I supposed to love mornings
when I have Mr. Zorn first hour?

But then if I stay home,
I'll miss music and English;
and Felicia will kill me
if I don't return her biology notes.
Oh, Lord, so much to think about
and try to figure out:
> Why didn't I do my homework?
> Why is French so hard for me?
> Does Mark like me or not?
> Why can't I lose weight
> or get along with my mother?
Lord, I love you,
but I'm sure I'm sick. Maybe I'll go back to sleep
and just miss first hour.[7]

> —Barbara (adolescent)

> Dear God,
> Is it true my father won't get in
> Heaven if he uses his bowling
> words in the house?[8]
> > —Anita (child)

Every day there are a zillion temptations, Lord.
It's *raining* sin out there,
and every time I step outside
I get pelted in the face
with dark invitations and
forbidden delights.
> "Just say no," they insist.
I try.
I turn away
but sometimes I feel deprived.
I get to thinking when I'm home alone,
and I wonder if I'm missing all the fun.
Can I be happy here

where you keep blessing me?
And will I be wise enough to stay here?[9]
—Becky (adolescent)

How did you know
you were God?[10]
—Charlie (child)

Lord, what's wrong with the people in my
church?
What happens to them when they get inside a
church?
They freeze up . . . they don't seem to enjoy
themselves or talk to anyone.
They look like penguins standing on the shore,
staring at the weary ocean.
. . . I watch them watching one another
as they waddle down the aisle, returning from a
sip of supermarket wine.
To be honest with you, God, I'm so thankful I'm
not like other people in church. . . .
I know quite well that I come to church and act
the part as others do.
But that's different, isn't it?
Or are other people in church like me anyway—
. . . Rebellious kids at heart, afraid to change the
way they act
In church because it's easier that way?[11]
—Matthew (adolescent)

Dear God,
Why is Sunday School on Sunday?
I thought it was suppose to be our day of rest.[12]
—Tom L. (child)

You know, Lord, how I serve you,
with great emotional fervor in the limelight.
You know how I bask in public ministry—
How my enthusiasm overflows at a Bible study.
But how would I react, I wonder,
if You pointed to a basin of water
and asked me to wash the calloused feet
of a bent and wrinkled old woman,
day after day, month after month,
in a room where nobody saw and nobody knew?[13]

—Ruth Harms Calkin (adapted)

God,
   Did you really mean "Do unto others as they do unto you"?
because if you did then I'm going to fix my brother.[14]

—Darla (child)

How long, O LORD, must I call for help,
   but you do not listen?
Or cry out to you, "Violence!"
   but you do not save?
Why do you make me look at injustice?
   Why do you tolerate wrong?

—Habakkuk
Habakkuk 1:2–3 NIV

Dear God,
Did you mean for [a] giraffe
to look like that or was it
   an accident?[15]

—Norma (child)

Why do I feel so sick inside,
so mad at myself?
. . . Why am I so confused
about what is right and about what is wrong?
God, if my parents ever knew

some of the things that go on in my head
I think they'd disown me.
They taught me the rules:
   Don't steal! Don't swear!
   Don't fight! Don't answer back!
And every time I break the rules
   I am guilty!
   I am wrong!
   I am bad!
I was born bad, they tell me,
and that's why I need the rules. . . .
Yes, the whole trouble with me is me.

I hate the rules
because, well, because they are just rules.
They are like squares on the floor,
like the circles of a target at the rifle range,
like lines running down the highway.
That's it!
They're like the lines on the highway,
   double yellow danger lines,
   and long white distance lines,
   and very hazy dotted lines
   that vanish in the rain. . . .
What if those targets were really faces?
And what if those lines were really lives?
And what if those rules were really people?
Then sin would be breaking people instead of breaking
   rules.
Sin would mean breaking up with God instead of breaking
   his laws.
Sin would be personal and cruel and wrong.

   Lord, why can't someone tell me what sin is all about?[16]
                              —Paul (adolescent)

Dear God,
How do you feel about people who
don't believe in you? Somebody
else wants to know.[17]

A friend,
Neil (child)

How long, O Lord? Will you forget me forever?
　　How long will you hide your face from me?
How long must I wrestle with my thoughts
　　and every day have sorrow in my heart?
　　How long will my enemy triumph over me?
Look on me and answer, O Lord my God.

—David
Psalm 13:1–3 NIV

Dear Lord,
　Do you have a long white beard? My grandfather said you
have a long white beard and I think he knows you.[18]

—Gwen [age 8]

7
Prayers for Children

For all these smallnesses
I thank You, Lord:

small children
and small needs;
small meals to cook,
small talk to heed,
and a small book
from which to read
small stories;
small hurts to heal,
small disappointments, too,
as real
as ours;
small glories
to discover
in bugs, pebbles, flowers.

When day is through my mind is small,
my strength is gone;
and as I gather
each dear one
I pray, "Bless each
for Jesus' sake—

such angels sleeping,
imps awake!"
What wears me out
are little things:
angels minus
shining wings.
Forgive me, Lord,
if I have whined;
. . . it takes so much
to keep them shined;
yet each small rub
has its reward,
for they have blessed *me*.
Thank You,
Lord.[1]

—Ruth Graham

This was written by Ruth while rearing her five children.

Seems like yesterday that he was handed to me in a blue blanket. Where have the years gone, Lord? I remember the way he cried while splashing buckets of water over a goldfish as it lay helpless on the kitchen floor, and the day he carried a tadpole home and sat down to watch it turn into a frog.

I remember long ago the rumpus he raised when the girl next door moved. And then suddenly he started practicing "America" when a marine moved in next door.

Then there were the laughs we had when he mowed the zigzag line down the yard and promised to buy me all the bubble gum in the world when he grew up. And it was exciting to watch his cycle of interests switch from Tinkertoys to intellectual activities.

Now here he is, Lord, so big and strong, and ready for the first grade.[2]

—Jeanette Struchen

O God, our Father,
The pain hurts very much.
Please help me to be brave,
But I know you will understand
If I have to cry.
Please help me do
What the doctor says to do,
And not make it harder
For those who take care of me.
And help me, dear God,
To go to sleep
And be better in the morning.[3]
　　—J. Ferguson (child's prayer)

Lord, help me to be more understanding of my children's limitations. Guard me against demanding more of them than they are equipped to give.

This son, so bright about anything mechanical, who's up half the night with his ham radio and is always grubby from rebuilding cars. Except for motoring magazines, he won't even read.

You know how hard I've tried—trips to the library, books of his own. I shudder at the memory, Lord, of my yelling and his furious, half-bitter, half-bewildered retorts. And that last accusation before he slammed off: "I can't help it, Mom. Stop trying to make me into something I'm not!"

Something he's not . . . and never will be. A professional man like his father. A lover of books and language like me. . . . How much he'll miss; my very soul grieves. But am I grieving so much for him as for myself?

The very idea of greasy engines is revolting to me—what if somebody tried to force me to build a radio? Help me to see his side of it, Lord, as I sit now in what seems the wreckage of my dreams for my son. Since you made him so different from us, you must have had your reasons. Help me to understand those reasons and release him to go his different way.

Dear Lord, instead of bemoaning my son's lacks, let me be grateful for his accomplishments. Give me new pride in them, and help me to convey that pride to him.

And my daughter, Lord. I just can't understand her anymore, and she can't understand me. We used to be so close—even when we had our differences she'd come flying back to me.

But now, though there are still moments of sweetness and laughter . . . those times are so few. I don't understand her silences, Lord, her locked door, the secrets she keeps from me. And when we do talk there is so much irritation, tension, and criticism. Where has my little girl gone, God? What have I done to drive her away?

You, Lord, seem to tell me that she's going where I went, where all girls go. Life is beckoning to her and she must follow. But it hurts, God. I love her so much. And clear and true I hear the answer: *Because it is so wonderful having a daughter, if this didn't happen you couldn't bear to let her go!*[4]

—Marjorie Holmes (excerpted)

Lord, who am I to teach the way
To little children day by day,
So prone myself to go astray?

I teach them knowledge, but I know
How faint they flicker, and how low
The candles of my knowledge glow.

I teach them power to will and do,
But only now to learn anew
My own great weakness through and through.

I teach them love for all mankind
And all God's creatures, but I find
My love comes lagging far behind.

Lord, if their guide I still must be,
O let the little children see
The teacher leaning hard on Thee.[5]

—Leslie Pinckney-Hill

Now I lay me down to sleep,
I pray Thee, Lord, Thy child to keep;
Thy love go with me all the night
And wake me with the morning light.

Now I lay me down to sleep,
I pray Thee, Lord, my soul to keep;
And should I die before I wake,
I trust Thee, Lord, my soul to take.[6]

—Anonymous

Lord, teach a little child to pray,
    And then accept my prayer,
For thou canst hear the words I say,
    For thou art everywhere.

A little sparrow cannot fall
    Unnoticed, Lord, by thee;
And though I am so young and small,
    Thou dost take care of me.

Teach me to do the thing that's right,
    And when I sin, forgive;
And make it still my chief delight
    To serve thee while I live.[7]

—Anonymous

Dear God,
Tommy is Your child, too.
So why can't I love him as I love the others?
There are times when I see a hungry look in his eyes,
That lost look;
That look that says he wants so desperately
To be loved and appreciated.
But most of the time, O God,
You know he comes into the room like a whirlwind,
Loud, and disruptive, and inconsiderate of others.

Most of the time I can give him special attention
And direct his boundless energy into a creative task.

But yesterday—Oh, yesterday
When he ran his black marker in squiggles
All over the Valentine bulletin board that
Jamie and Anne had worked so hard to decorate for our
party,
I'm afraid I forgot all about positive reinforcement,
And ignoring negative behavior, and all those
Good modeling techniques I had learned to practice.
    In a word, I *blew up* and the whole class saw
    That other side of me.

Forgive me, dear God,
Help the children to forgive me,
And help me to forgive myself, and to grow through this
    experience,
And to learn to show my love to Tommy
Even as You would have me love this special child of Yours.[8]
                                        —Helen Monroe

God of the lost and the little,
I rejoice when some are found!
There are too many in this world
who have no sense of direction,
who listen to the misleading guidance of others,
and who wind up in places
where they really should not go.
Too many adults, Lord,
are too childish to be parents.
They are not responsible,
or their burdens are too much for them to bear.
Thinking of themselves first,
they forget the children
and abuse them through neglect.
Too many children, Lord,
have grown up too fast.

They must give up their innocence,
never to get it back.
Too many parents, Lord,
never fully know what is happening with their children.
They have lost them somehow
in the difficult maze of living a life
that has too much neglect and too much selfishness.
Yet sometimes, O Lord,
little ones are found!
And the rejoicing in heaven
seems little match for the rejoicing
that is felt on earth![9]

—Micheal Elliott

Dear God, there are so many questions as the children leave the room today.
Have they had a good day?
Will Susan have any supper tonight—or breakfast tomorrow?
What should I do about the hours she spends alone?
Has Mike's father returned home—why is Mike so quiet?
Why won't Gerri ever be quiet?
What kind of day has my son had—
Does his teacher realize that though he doesn't
express his thoughts well in words,
he expresses himself in his drawing?
What will we have for supper?
Have the children seen Christ in me today?
So many questions as the children leave.

Help me remember, God, that the answer to all the questions is you and my personal experience of you. It is your indwelling presence in me that can help me understand the answers. It is the certainty of your ever-present Spirit that helps me understand, too, that the questions I cannot put into words can be answered. Guide me through each day; give me the wisdom to ask the questions I feel and the courage to follow where your answers lead. In the name of the indwelling Christ, I pray.[10]

—Martha Hazzard (schoolteacher)

God, give me the strength to discipline my children. Give me the love and the courage to lay down rules and see that they abide by them. Give me the ability to say *no* when all my being longs to yield just because they want me to so much, or because I'd spare myself a lot of misery by saying *yes*.

Lord, help me to remember that children need the barriers of discipline to protect them from a world they're not yet ready for. And however loud they howl about "maturity" and "all the other kids" and "you don't trust me" and "you want to keep me a baby," in their secret hearts they're often thankful that the barriers are there. Even proud of having parents who care enough about them to say "No, you can't" and mean it. Help me to remember that this sort of caring gives them a sense of value that no amount of weak-kneed yielding to their every impassioned plea can match.

But oh, Lord, give me judgment in discipline so that I don't become a tyrant. Never let me discipline out of a sense of power and authority rather than a genuine concern for the welfare and happiness of my children. Give me understanding, too, and a sense of humor and fair play. Make me strong in discipline, Lord, but make me wise as well.[11]

—Marjorie Holmes

> Father, hear us, we are praying,
> Hear the words our hearts are saying,
> We are praying for our children.
>
> Keep them from the powers of evil,
> From the secret, hidden peril,
> From the whirlpool that would suck them,
> From the treacherous quicksand pluck them.
>
> From the worldling's hollow gladness,
> From the sting of faithless sadness,
> Holy Father, save our children.

Through life's troubled waters steer them,
Through life's bitter battle cheer them,
Father, Father, be Thou near them.
Read the language of our longing,
Read the wordless pleadings thronging,
Holy Father, for our children.
  And wherever they may bide,
  Lead them Home at eventide.[12]
                              —Amy Carmichael

For several decades, Carmichael cared for abused and abandoned children in India.

When a young boy cries
in bed at night,
stealthily,
silently,
never aloud,
newly away
from family and friends,
too old to cry,
too proud;
too young to know
each night passes on
making way
for a newer dawn;
too old
to stay
in the nest, and yet
too young
to fly
away.

God,
be near
when a young boy cries.[13]
                              —Ruth Graham

8

Prayers of Confession

Jesus, you are Lord of my life. I don't know why I do some of the things I do. I lose my temper and swear and fight with my sisters. . . .

Lord, I have so many bad habits. I'm like that dying seal I saw last week at the beach—out of the water and gasping for breath on dry, hot sand.

I was born to know you and serve you, but sometimes I just don't act anything at all like a Christian. Your Word says I have a new nature, and I want to live like it. Your Word says to count myself dead to sin and alive to you. I want to! Please channel my temperament to your glory, and help me to understand myself in the light of your Word, so bad habits won't defeat me and separate me from you.[1]

—James (adolescent)

Ah dearest Lord! I cannot pray,
    My fancy is not free;
Unmannerly distractions come,
    And force my thoughts from Thee.

The world that looks so dull all day
    Glows bright on me at prayer,
And plans that ask no thought but then
    Wake up and meet me there.

Old voices murmur in my ear,
  New hopes spring up to life,
And past and future gaily blend
  In one bewitching strife.

My very flesh has restless fits;
  My changeful limbs conspire
With all these phantoms of the mind
  My inner self to tire.

Sweet Jesus! teach me how to prize
  These tedious hours when I,
Foolish and mute before Thy face,
  In helpless worship lie.

For Thou art oft most present, Lord!
  In weak distracted prayer:
A sinner out of heart with self
  Most often finds Thee there.

These surface troubles come and go,
  Like rufflings of the sea;
The deeper depth is out of reach
  To all, my God, but Thee.[2]

—F. W. Faber

Lord, I detest myself right now. I've just come from a luncheon where four of us spent most of our time criticizing a mutual friend. Her faults, her eccentricities, how extravagant and undependable she is. How she spoils her children, how vain and eager she always is to be attractive to men.

And though a lot of these things are true, I found myself wondering even as I joined in, *Who are we to judge?* Isn't every one of us guilty of at least some of the very same things? Was that why we attacked her with such relish? Because it made us feel a little bit better ourselves to brandish the defects of somebody so much "worse."

I keep thinking of what Jesus said to the men about to stone the adulterous woman: "Which of you is without sin?" Yet there we sat, self-righteous, stoning our sister with words.

How, Lord, can I make amends? I long to call her up and beg her forgiveness, but that would be a terrible mistake. She'd be so hurt, so much damage would be done. No, all I can do is ask your forgiveness. And pray for her. Help her, strengthen her, bless her. Don't let her ever know what we said about her. And oh, Lord, put more compassion in my heart. Don't let me ever again join in stoning a sister—or anyone—with words.[3]

—Marjorie Holmes (excerpted)

> Because I spent the strength Thou gavest me
> In struggle which Thou never didst ordain,
> And have but dregs of life to offer Thee—
> O Lord, I do repent.[4]
>
> —Sarah Williams

Almighty God, we have come a long way since our birth as a republic, but we have wandered somehow. Our Founding Fathers held freedom of religion as fundamental. We have translated their deep conviction into freedom from religion.

We have become technological giants, and spiritual and moral dwarfs. We are sophisticated in scientific progress and primitive in spiritual development.

We are knowledgeable in the ways of the world and ignorant in the ways of God. We live as though man is the center of the universe and You a peripheral invention of pious enthusiasts.

We are abundantly rich in material resources and abysmally poor in spiritual and moral capital.

Dear God, help us get our act together before it is too late. In the name of Him who is the Way, the Truth, and the Life.[5]

—Richard Halverson, Chaplain
United States Senate

Have mercy on me, O God,
  according to your unfailing love;
according to your great compassion
  blot out my transgressions.
Wash away all my iniquity
  and cleanse me from my sin.

For I know my transgressions,
  and my sin is always before me.
Against you, you only, have I sinned
  and done what is evil in your sight,
so that you are proved right when you speak
  and justified when you judge.
Surely I was sinful at birth,
  sinful from the time my mother conceived me. . . .

Cleanse me with hyssop, and I will be clean;
  wash me and I will be whiter than snow. . . .

Create in me a pure heart, O God,
  and renew a steadfast spirit within me.
Do not cast me from your presence
  or take your Holy Spirit from me.
Restore to me the joy of your salvation
  and grant me a willing spirit to sustain me.

Then will I teach transgressors your ways,
  and sinners will turn back to you.

—King David
Psalm 51 NIV

   This excerpt is from a confession that David prayed after he committed adultery with Bathsheba and arranged the murder of Bathsheba's husband.

Too well, O Christ, we know Thee;
On our eyes there sits a film
Through which we dimly see
Of frozen faith and stagnant memory.
Thou art among us in the homely guise
Of One whose nearness, like a shadow, lies
Between our minds and His own mystery;
And our familiar knowledge is to Thee
A second tomb, from which Thou canst not rise.

Thou hast a sepulchre not made with hands,
Built of our stale beliefs, and we lay there
Our formal wreaths of customary prayer.
But in that hollow place no angel stands;
It is not visions that our faith demands,
But plain instruction from the Gardener.[6]

—Handley Jones

O tenderest Love,
how we do fail
through our own folly
to avail
ourselves of You.
Cold,
we shun
Your warmth,
Your sun;
dry,
Your dew,
Your everflowing Spring;
and pressured much,
we miss Your gentle,
calming touch;
then wonder, "Why?"
O pitying Heart,
forgive
the pauper spirit

that would live
a beggar
at Your Open Gate
until it is too late
—too late.[7]
    —Ruth Graham

Our Father who is in heaven,
and here on earth too,
waiting to be heard,
waiting to be seen,
as we say the words
and go through the motions we have learned—
break through to us somehow.
We are too busy praying
to really communicate with you.
Our prayers are monologues
and not dialogues.
I have too much I want to say
so that I do not take the time to hear
what you want to say to me.
I do not sense your presence
when it passes by me.

I thank you for these times
and desire they happen more often,
but right now I am in a hurry.
I have to attend another banquet—
I have been asked to say grace.[8]
    —Micheal Elliott

Thou hidden Source of calm repose,
Thou all-sufficient Love divine,
My help and refuge from my foes,
Secure I am, if Thou art mine;
And lo! from sin, and grief, and shame,
I hide me, Jesus, in Thy name.

Jesus, my all in all Thou art,
My rest in toil, my ease in pain,
The medicine of my broken heart—
In war my peace, in loss my gain,
My smile beneath the tyrant's frown,
In shame my glory and my crown.

In want my plentiful supply,
In weakness my almighty power;
In bonds my perfect liberty,
My light in Satan's darkest hour,
My joy in grief, my shield in strife,
In death my everlasting life.[9]

     —Charles Wesley

O LORD, God of heaven, the great and awesome God, who keeps his covenant of love with those who love him and obey his commands, let your ear be attentive and your eyes open to hear the prayer your servant is praying before you day and night for your servants, the people of Israel. I confess the sins we Israelites, including myself and my father's house, have committed against you. We have acted very wickedly toward you. We have not obeyed the commands, decrees and laws you gave your servant Moses.

Remember the instruction you gave your servant Moses, saying, "If you are unfaithful, I will scatter you among the nations, but if you return to me and obey my commands, then even if your exiled people are at the farthest horizon, I will gather them from there and bring them to the place I have chosen as a dwelling for my Name." They are your servants and your people, whom you redeemed by your great strength and your mighty hand. O Lord, let your ear be attentive to the prayer of this your servant and to the prayer of your servants who delight in revering your name. Give your servant success today by granting him favor in the presence of this man [the king].

     —Nehemiah
     Nehemiah 1:5–11 NIV

Nehemiah spoke this prayer as he agonized over the broken down walls of Jerusalem and contemplated requesting permission from the king of Persia to rebuild.

Lord, we admit to ourselves and to you that we have often enjoyed our faith and the privilege of being your people, while avoiding the responsibility for making our spiritual discoveries known to others.

Our lives should be living illustrations of the truth, but they are frequently hard to read and even sometimes misleading. We are often too busy to think through our faith and to be prepared to give a defense of our position and an introduction to the Savior. We are fearful of rejection and even of being thought different. We consign to professional people in the church the task that belongs to us all, of recommending the Master to the man on the street.

We are unwilling to suffer even slight inconvenience that someone else may turn from a meaningless existence to purposeful living. And sometimes with lop-sided concern we pray too much for our loved ones and insufficiently for your loved ones—the poor, the defenseless, the neglected little people of the world. Too often, Lord, we try to predict who will respond and who will not, and we recommend with presumptive rashness when and how you are to fulfill our prayers for the salvation of others. Father, forgive these wrong and unhealthy attitudes.

Help us to love you so ardently and so courageously that, with tact and a sense of humor and great graciousness, we may begin to find all sorts of opportunities to recommend you to those who desperately need you.[10]

—Bryan Jeffery Leech

O Jesus, my feet are dirty. Come even as a slave to me, pour water into your bowl, come and wash my feet. In asking such a thing I know I am overbold but I dread what was threatened when you said to me, "If I do not wash your feet, I have no fellowship with you."

Wash my feet then, because I long for your companion-
ship. And yet, what am I asking? It was well for Peter to ask
you to wash his feet. For him that was all that was needed for
him to be clean in every part. With me it is different; though
you wash me now, I shall still stand in need of that other washing, the cleansing you promised when you said, "There is a
baptism I must needs be baptized with."[11]

                                                    —Origen

        O Lord,
            in whose hands are life and death,
            by whose power I am sustained,
            and by whose mercy I am spared,
            look down upon me with pity.

        Forgive me that I have
            until now so much neglected the duty
            which Thou hast assigned to me,
            and suffered the days and hours
            of which I must give account
            to pass away without any endeavor
            to accomplish Thy will.

        Make me to remember, O God, that
            every day is Thy gift and ought
            to be used according to Thy command.
        Grant me, therefore,
            so to repent of my negligence
            that I may obtain mercy from Thee, and
            pass the time which Thou shalt yet allow me
            in diligent performance of Thy commands,
            through Jesus Christ.[12]

                                        —Samuel Johnson

O heavenly Father, we have loved Thee but not enough, we
have sought Thee but not diligently, we have seen but not perceived, we have heard but not understood, we have hoped for

things heavenly, but clung to things of earth, and our hearts have been far from Thee, the Holy One. Draw them now in mercy unto Thyself, O God, that the time to come be not as the past, but that, finding, perceiving, understanding, and loving Thee, we may have rest and joy undisturbed forevermore.[13]

—Anonymous

O Lord, remember not only the men and women of good will, but also those of ill will. But do not remember all the suffering they have inflicted on us; remember the fruits we have bought, thanks to this suffering—our comradeship, our loyalty, our courage, our generosity, the greatness of heart which has grown out of all this, and when they come to judgment let all the fruits which we have borne be their forgiveness.[14]

—Unknown Prisoner

This prayer was written by a prisoner in Ravensbruck concentration camp and was left by the body of a dead child.

I confess, O God—that often I let my mind wander down unclean and forbidden ways; that often I deceive myself as to where my plain duty lies; that often, by concealing my real motives, I pretend to be better than I am; that often my honesty is only a matter of policy; that often my affection for my friends is only a refined form of caring for myself; that often my sparing of my enemy is due to nothing more than cowardice; that often I do good deeds only that they may be seen of men, and shun evil ones only because I fear they may be found out.

O Holy One, let the fire of thy love enter my heart, and burn up all this coil of meanness and hypocrisy, and make my heart as the heart of a little child.[15]

—John Baille

O God, our leader and master and our friend, forgive our imperfections and our little motives; take us and make us one with Thy great purpose, use us and do not reject us, make us

all servants of Thy kingdom. Weave our lives into Thy struggle to conquer and to bring peace and union to the world.

We are small and feeble creatures; we are feeble in speech, feebler still in action, nevertheless let but Thy light shine upon us, and there is not one of us who cannot be lit by Thy fire and who cannot lose himself in Thy salvation. Take us into Thy purposes, O God. Let Thy kingdom come into our hearts and into this world.[16]

—H. G. Wells

O God, forgive that now I live
As if I might, sometime, return
To bless the weary ones that yearn
For help and comfort every day—
For there be such along the way.
O God, forgive that I have seen
The beauty only, have not been
Awake to sorrow such as this;
That I have drunk the cup of bliss
Remembering not that those there be
Who drink the dregs of misery.
I love the beauty of the scene,
Would roam again o'er fields so green;
But since I may not, let me spend
My strength for others to the end—
For those who tread on rock and stone,
And bear their burdens all alone,
Who loiter not in leafy bowers,
Nor hear the birds nor pluck the flowers.
A larger kindness give to me,
A deeper love and sympathy;
 Then, O, one day
 May someone say—
Remembering a lessened pain:
"Would she could pass this way again."[17]

—Eva Rose York

If my soul has turned perversely to the dark;
If I have left some brother wounded by the way;
If I have preferred my aims to Thine;
If I have been impatient and would not wait;
If I have marred the pattern drawn out for my life;
If I have cost tears to those I loved;
If my heart has murmured against Thy will,
O Lord, forgive.[18]

—F. B. Meyer

My eyes are dry, my faith is old,
My heart is hard, my prayers are cold.
And I know how I ought to be—
Alive to You and dead to me.
Oh, what can be done with an old heart like mine?
Soften it up with oil and wine!
The oil is You, Your Spirit of love,
Please wash me anew in the wine of Your blood.[19]

—Keith Green

Almighty and everlasting God,
you hate nothing that you have made,
and forgive the sins of all those who are penitent.
Create and make in us new and contrite hearts,
that, lamenting our sins
and acknowledging our wretchedness,
we may receive from you, the God of all mercy,
perfect forgiveness and peace;
through Jesus Christ our Lord,
Amen.[20]

—Thomas Cranmer

Cranmer ordered that an English translation of the Bible should be placed in every church and read aloud regularly. He also compiled the immensely popular *Book of Common Prayer.* He was later martyred under Mary Tudor.

From all my lame defeats and oh! much more
    From all the victories that I seemed to score;
From cleverness shot forth on Thy behalf
    At which, while angels weep, the audience laugh;
From all my proofs of Thy divinity,
    Thou, who wouldst give no sign, deliver me.

Thoughts are but coins. Let me not trust, instead
    Of thee, their thin-worn image of Thy head.
From all my thoughts, even from my thoughts of Thee,
    O thou fair Silence, fall, and set me free.
Lord of the narrow gate and the needle's eye,
    Take from me all my trumpery least I die.[21]

                                           —C. S. Lewis

Forgive us, O God, for our small concept of the heart of the Eternal, for the doubting suspicion with which we regard the heart of God.

    Give to us more faith. We have so little, we say. Yet we have faith in each other—in checks and banks, in trains and airplanes, in cooks, and in strangers who drive us in cabs. Forgive us for our stupidity, that we have faith in people whom we do not know, and are so reluctant to have faith in Thee who knowest us altogether.

    We are always striving to find a complicated way through life when Thou hast a plan, and we refuse to walk in it. So many of our troubles we bring on ourselves. How silly we are. . . .

    Wilt thou give to us that faith that we can deposit in the bank of Thy love, so that we may receive the dividends and interest that Thou art so willing to give us. We ask it all in the lovely name of Jesus Christ our Savior. Amen.[22]

                                      —Peter Marshall

I know that you can do all things;
   no plan of yours can be thwarted.
You asked, "Who is this that obscures my counsel
   without knowledge?"
Surely I spoke of things I did not understand,
   things too wonderful for me to know.

You said, "Listen now, and I will speak;
   I will question you,
   and you shall answer me."
My ears had heard of you
   but now my eyes have seen you.
Therefore I despise myself
   and repent in dust and ashes.

—Job
Job 42:2–6 NIV

Job uttered this prayer following God's tumultuous reply to his
pleadings.

Father, those who deny Thee could not deny, if Thou
   didst not exist;
and their denial is never complete, for if it were so,
   they would not exist.
They affirm Thee in living; all things affirm Thee in
   living;
the bird in the air, both the hawk and the finch;
the beast on the earth, both the wolf and the lamb. . . .
Therefore man, whom Thou hast made to be conscious
   of Thee,
must consciously praise Thee, in thought and in word
   and in deed.

We thank Thee for Thy mercies of blood, for Thy redemption by blood;
For the blood of Thy martyrs and saints shall enrich
   the earth, shall create the holy places.

For wherever a saint has dwelt, wherever a martyr has
given his blood for the blood of Christ,
there is holy ground, and the sanctity shall not depart
from it.
Though armies trample over it, though sightseers come
with guidebooks looking over it.

Forgive us, O Lord, we acknowledge ourselves as type
of the common man,
Of the men and women who shut the door and sit by
the fire.
Who fear the blessing of God, the loneliness of the
night of God,
the surrender required, the deprivation inflicted.
Who fear the injustice of men less than the justice of
God;
Who fear the hand at the window, the fire in the thatch,
the fist in the tavern, the push into the canal
Less than we fear the love of God.

We acknowledge our trespass, our weakness, our fault;
We acknowledge that the sin of the world is upon our
heads;
that the blood of the martyrs and the saints is upon
our heads.
Lord, have mercy upon us.
Christ, have mercy upon us.
Lord, have mercy upon us.[23]

—adapted from T. S. Eliot

O sacred Head, now wounded, with grief and shame weighed
down,
Now scornfully surrounded with thorns, Thine only crown;
O sacred Head, what glory, what bliss till now was Thine!
Yet, though despised and gory, I joy to call Thee mine.

What Thou, my Lord, hast suffered was all for sinners' gain;
Mine, mine was the transgression, but Thine the deadly pain.
Lo, here I fall, my Savior! 'Tis I deserve Thy place;
Look on me with Thy favor, vouchsafe to me Thy grace.

What language shall I borrow to thank Thee, dearest Friend;
For this Thy dying sorrow, Thy pity without end?
O make me Thine forever, and should I fainting be,
Lord, let me never, never outlive my love to Thee.

Be near me when I'm dying, O show Thy cross to me;
And for my succor flying, come, Lord, to set me free.
These eyes, new faith receiving, from Jesus shall not move;
For he who dies believing, dies safely through Thy love.[24]

—Written by Hans Leo Hassler;
arranged by Johann Sebastian Bach
the year before his death

Almighty and most merciful Father,
We have erred and strayed from Thy ways like lost sheep.
We have followed too much the devices and desires of our own
hearts;
We have left undone those things which we ought to have done;
And we have done those things which we ought not to have done;
And there is no health in us.
But, Thou, O Lord have mercy upon us miserable offenders;
Spare Thou those, O God, who confess their faults,
Restore Thou those who are penitent according to Thy promises
Declared unto mankind in Christ Jesus our Lord;
And grant, O most merciful Father, for his sake
That we may hereafter live a godly, righteous and sober life,
To the glory of Thy holy name.[25]

—*The Book of Common Prayer*

9

Prayers of Consecration

Do you, my God, stand by me, against all the world's wisdom and reason. . . . I would prefer to have peaceful days and to be out of this turmoil. But yours, O Lord, is this cause. . . . Stand by me, O God, in the name of your dear Son, Jesus Christ, who shall be my Defense and Shelter, yes, my Mighty Fortress through the might and strength of your Holy Spirit.[1]

—Martin Luther

Use me, my Savior, for whatever purpose and in whatever way you may require. Here is my poor heart, an empty vessel: fill it with your grace. Here is my sinful and troubled soul; quicken it and refresh it with your love. Take my heart for your abode; my mouth to spread abroad the glory of your name; my love and all my powers for the advancement of your believing people, and never allow the steadfastness and confidence of my faith to abate.[2]

—Dwight L. Moody

My Jesus, my King, my life, my all. I again dedicate my whole
self to Thee. Accept me and grant, O gracious Father, that ere
this year is gone I may finish my task. In Jesus' name I ask it.[3]

—David Livingstone

Livingstone made this entry in his diary during the year before he
was found dead, kneeling beside his cot in Africa.

> Put out my eyes, and I can see You still;
> slam my ears too, and I can hear You yet;
> and without my feet can go to You;
> and tongueless, I can conjure You at will.
> Break off my arms, I shall take hold of You
> and grasp You with my heart as with a hand;
> arrest my heart, my brain will beat as true;
> and if you set this brain of mine afire,
> then on my bloodstream I will carry You.[4]
>
> —Rainer Maria Rilke

Here I am, O God, of little power and of mean estate, yet lifting up heart and voice to thee before whom all created things
are as dust and a vapor. Thou art hidden behind the curtain of
sense, incomprehensible in thy greatness, mysterious in thine
almighty power; yet here I speak with thee familiarly as child
to parent, as friend to friend. If I could not thus speak to thee,
then were I indeed without hope in the world.

It is little that I have power to do or to ordain. Not of my
own will am I here, not of my own will shall I soon pass hence.
Of all that shall come to me this day, very little will be such as
I have chosen for myself. It is thou, O hidden One, who dost
appoint my lot and determine the bounds of my habitation.
It is thou who hast put power in my hand to do one work and
hast withheld the skill to do another. It is thou who dost keep
in thy grasp the threads of this day's life and who alone knowest
what lies before me to do or to suffer.

But because thou art my Father, I am not afraid. Because it
is thine own Spirit that stirs within my spirit's inmost room, I

know that all is well. What I desire for myself I cannot attain, but what thou desirest in me thou canst attain for me. Make this day's work a little part of the work of the kingdom of my Lord Christ, in whose name these my prayers are said.[5]

—John Baille

Lord, who am I to teach the way
To little children day by day,
So prone myself to go astray?

I teach them knowledge, but I know
How faint they flicker, and how low
The candles of my knowledge glow.

I teach them power to will and do,
But only now to learn anew
My own great weakness through and through.

I teach them love for all mankind
And all God's creatures, but I find
My love comes lagging far behind.

Lord, if their guide I still must be,
O let the little children see
The teacher leaning hard on Thee.[6]

—Leslie Pinckney-Hill

If you can do anything with this life, Jesus, go ahead and do it. I'm messed up. I don't have no place to go. I hate my father. I hate my mother. I even hate myself. Please, for God's sake, if there's anything you can do, do it![7]

—New York City teen

After another day of trying to evangelize defiant street kids, Bill Milliken overheard the above prayer coming from a dark room.

Drop Thy still dews of quietness,
　　Till all our strivings cease;
Take from our souls the strain and stress,
　　And let our ordered lives confess
The beauty of Thy peace.[8]

—J. G. Whittier

O Lord, take up the slack in me.
There is so much of me that loosely dangles without purpose.
Blow away the feathers in my head.
Get me off this binge of insensitivity.
Yank the blinders that keep me peeking at the world.
Never let me get so old that I can't feel growing pains,
Or stay so young that somebody else shoulders my
　　responsibility.
Shake the starch out of my mind and put it in my backbone.
Erase the wings from my tongue and hitch them to my actions.[9]

—Jeanette Struchen

To Thee we give ourselves today,
Forgetful of the world outside;
We tarry in Thy house, O Lord,
From eventide to eventide.

From Thy all-searching, righteous eye
Our deepest heart can nothing hide;
It crieth up to Thee for peace
From eventide to eventide.

Who could endure, should'st Thou, O God,
As we deserve, forever chide!
We therefore seek Thy pardoning grace
From eventide to eventide.

O may we lay to heart how swift
The years of life do onward glide;

So learn to live that we may see
Thy light at our life's eventide.[10]
—Gustav Gottheil

The embers of the day are red
Beyond the murky hill.
The kitchen smokes; the bed
In the darkling house is spread:
The great sky darkens overhead,
And the great woods are shrill.
So far have I been led,
Lord, by Thy will:
So far I have followed, Lord, and wondered still.
The breeze from the embalmed land
Blows sudden towards the shore,
And claps my cottage door.
I hear the signal, Lord—I understand.
The night at Thy command
Comes. I will eat and sleep and will not question more.[11]
—Robert Louis Stevenson

I receive Thee, Price of my redemption. . . . for love of whom I
have studied and watched, toiled, preached, and taught. Never
have I said anything against Thee; but if I have done so, it is
through ignorance, and I do not persist in my opinions. . . .
—Thomas Aquinas

Though critics called him "Dumb Ox" for his slow manner,
Aquinas's quick mind earned him respect as a theologian and phi-
losopher in the 1200s.

Christ protect me today
    against poison, against burning,
    against drowning, against wounding,
    so that there may come abundance of reward.
Christ with me, Christ before me, Christ behind me,
Christ in me, Christ beneath me, Christ above me,

Christ on my right, Christ on my left,
Christ where I lie, Christ where I sit, Christ where I arise,
Christ in the heart of every man who thinks of me,
Christ in the mouth of every man who speaks to me,
Christ in every eye that sees me,
Christ in every ear that hears me.

I arise today
 through a mighty strength, the invocation of the Trinity,
 through belief in Threeness,
 through confession of the Oneness
 towards the Creator.
Salvation is of the Lord.
Salvation is of the Lord.
Salvation is of the Lord.
May thy salvation, O Lord, be ever with us.[12]
—St. Patrick (excerpted)

Sever me from myself that I may be grateful to you;
may I perish to myself that I may be safe in you;
may I die to myself that I may live in you;
may I be emptied of myself that I may abound in you;
may I be nothing to myself that I may be all to you.[13]
—Desiderius Erasmus

Erasmus was a leading scholar in the fifteenth and sixteenth centuries. He wrote powerfully against corruption in the Catholic church but never officially joined the Protestant cause.

Lord God and Father, I call upon Thee to enter all the avenues of my life today and to share every detail of it with me. Even as Thou hast called me to share with Thee Thy life, and all the wonders of it. As I am entering Thy treasures, Thou must now come in to possess all mine. As I am to share the destiny, glory, and future affairs of Thy Son, so would I now have Him share this small destiny of earth which is mine, the joys of it, and all

its small matters—that we should be One, Thou and I, even as we are in Christ.[14]

—Jim Elliot

Elliot wrote this prayer in his diary shortly before his martyrdom in Ecuador by members of the Auca Indian Tribe.

> Take the tiny stones which I have wrought,
> Just one by one, as they were giv'n by Thee,
> Not knowing what came next in Thy wise thought.
> Set each stone by Thy Master-hand of grace;
> Form the mosaic as Thou wilt for me,
> And in Thy temple pavement give it place.[15]
>
> —Frances Ridley Havergal

When I survey the evils of this world in which we thy servants live, and behold the doings of the wicked—the hate of enemies, the dangers and crafty machinations of the impious and by which we are continually endangered, yet even more when I remember my own life, how many errors and faults have beset me from my youth, I am afraid. I am ashamed and full of despondency. But as soon as I reflect again on thy mighty hand, the greatness and the continuity of thy assistance to me, I resume again my power of reasoning and become more elevated in my hopes. For this reason, coming to thee now with humble heart, I thank thee . . . for all the blessings which thou hast granted to me, thou who, having preserved me from such great dangers and exalted me to the royal throne of this kingdom, hast not ceased to guard me upon it. . . .

Wherefore, confiding in thy unspeakable goodness, I approach and pray thee. . . . my master, my deliverer, King of the universe: sanctify me in soul and in body, in mind and in heart, and renew me wholly. And be to me a helper and protector, ruling in peace my life and my people, thou who alone art blessed everywhere now and for endless ages.[16]

—Queen Elizabeth I

Eternal God, who hast formed all hearts to love thee and created all desires to be unsatisfied save in thee, quicken within our souls a continuing longing to worship thee. Wherever we may be, enable us to draw near to thee in spirit and in truth. In quietness and confidence we would open the door that thou mayest enter. Do for us what we cannot do for ourselves.

We bring to thee our consciences, dulled and insensitive. Quicken them by thy holiness. We bring to thee our minds, captured by the trivial and partial. Feed them with thy truth. We lift before thee our imaginations, stained by impurity. Purge them by thy beauty. We lift our hearts, wherein selfishness dwells. Open them to thy love. Into thy hands we place our wayward wills. Fashion them to thy purpose.

Send us from our worship into the affairs of life so strengthened within by thy Spirit that we may be co-workers with thee, revealed in Jesus Christ our Lord.[17]

—W. W. Anderson

Jesus, I am resting, resting
   In the joy of what Thou art,
I am finding out the greatness
   Of Thy loving heart.
Here I gaze and gaze upon Thee,
   As Thy beauty fills my soul,
For by Thy transforming power,
   Thou hast made me whole.

O how great Thy lovingkindness,
   Vaster, broader than the sea;
O how marvellous Thy goodness
   Lavished all on me—
Yes, I rest in Thee, Beloved,
   Know what wealth of grace is Thine,
Know Thy certainty of promise
   And have made it mine.

Simply trusting Thee, Lord Jesus,
   I behold Thee as Thou art,
And Thy love, so pure, so changeless,
   Satisfies my heart,
Satisfies its deepest longing,
   Meets, supplies my every need,
Compasseth me round with blessings;
   Thine is love indeed.

Ever lift Thy face upon me,
   As I work and wait for Thee;
Resting 'neath Thy smile, Lord Jesus,
   Earth's dark shadows flee.
Brightness of my Father's glory,
   Sunshine of my Father's face,
Let Thy glory e'er shine on me,
   Fill me with Thy grace.[18]
              —Jean Sophia Pigott

Father, bless to our hearts this word from your Word.
Help us to make our lives count for you.
Help us to serve you with the strength of youth,
. . . and the strength of age.
And take us at last into your presence,
Through Jesus Christ our Lord.[19]
              —Dr. Louis Benes

Dr. Benes spoke this prayer at the close of a sermon he preached in his pulpit at Garfield Park Reformed Church in Michigan. Moments later he died from a heart attack.

Bridler of colts untamed,
Over our wills preside;
Winger of wandering birds,
Our flight securely guide.
Rudder of youth unbending,
firm against adverse shock;

Shepherd, with wisdom tend the
Lambs of the royal flock:
Thy simple children bring
In one, that we may sing
In solemn lays
Our hymns of praise
With guileless lips to Christ our King.[20]
  —Clement of Alexandria (adapted)

Lord, I give up all my own plans and purposes,
All my own desires and hopes
And accept Thy will for my life.
I give myself, my life, my all,
Utterly to Thee to be Thine forever.
Fill me and seal me with Thy Holy Spirit,
Use me as Thou wilt,
Send me where Thou wilt,
Work out Thy whole will in my life
At any cost now and forever.[21]

      —Betty Stam

Stam was a missionary who, with her husband, was beheaded in 1934 by Chinese Communist guerrillas.

Make me a captive, Lord,
And then I shall be free;
Force me to render up my sword,
And I shall conqueror be.
I sink in life's alarms
When by myself I stand;
Imprison me within Thine arms,
And strong shall be my hand.

My heart is weak and poor
Until it master find;
It has no spring of action sure—
It varies with the wind;

It cannot freely move
Till Thou hast wrought its chain;
Enslave it with Thy matchless love,
And deathless it shall reign.

My power is faint and low
Till I have learned to serve;
It wants the needed fire to glow,
It wants the breeze to nerve;
It cannot drive the world
Until itself be driven;
Its flag can only be unfurled
When Thou shalt breathe from heaven.

My will is not my own
Till Thou hast made it Thine;
If it would reach a monarch's throne
It must its crown resign;
It only stands unbent
Amid the clashing strife,
When on Thy bosom it has leant
And found in Thee its life.[22]

—George Matheson

O thou Good Omnipotent, who so carest for every one of us as if thou carest for him alone, and so for all as if all were but one. Blessed is the one who loveth Thee, and his friend in Thee, and his enemy for Thee. For he only loses none dear to him to whom all are dear in You, who cannot be lost. So who is that but our God, the God that made heaven and earth, and filleth them, even by creating them. And Thy law is truth, and truth is Thyself.

I behold now some things pass away that others may replace them, but Thou dost never depart, O God, my Father supremely good—beauty of all things beautiful. To Thee will I entrust whatsoever I have received from Thee; so shall I lose nothing. Thou madest me for Thyself, and my heart is restless until it repose in Thee.[23]

—Augustine of Hippo

But if distractions manifold prevail,
And if in this we must confess we fail,
Grant us to keep at least a prompt desire,
An altar heaped and waiting to take fire
With the least spark, and leap into a blaze.[24]
—Richard Trench

God,
I heard today
Of a decrepit native woman
Who walked mile after mile
Under the blistering sun
To bring a small gift of embroidery
To the missionary she deeply loved.
Hour after hour she trudged
Over rough, rugged roads
Clutching tightly her small gift.
Her weary body sagged
Her vision blurred
Her bare feet bled from jagged rocks.

Grateful but overwhelmed
The missionary wept.
The trembling old woman spoke softly:
    "P-Please understand . . .
    the walk is a part of the gift."

My Lord,
My commitment to You is for life.
I give myself to You unreservedly
To do with me as You please.
But may I not forget
That the tears, the fears
The strain and the pain
The sunless days
The starless nights
Are all a part of the whole—

In my total commitment
I give full consent:
The walk is part of the gift.[25]
 —Ruth Harms Calkin

When I have nothing in my hand
  Wherewith to serve my King,
When Thy commandment finds me weak
  And wanting everything,
My soul, upon Thy greatness cast,
  Shall rise divinely free;
Then will I serve with what Thou hast,
  And gird myself with Thee.[26]
 —Anna Waring

Lord, when the sense of Thy sweet grace
Sends up my soul to seek Thy face,
Thy blessed eyes breed such desire,
I die in love's delicious Fire.
  O Love, I am thy sacrifice.
Be still triumphant, blessed eyes.
Yet shine on me, fair suns! That I
Still may behold, though still I die.

Though still I die, I live again;
Still longing so to be yet slain,
So gainful is such loss of breath.
I die e'en in desire of breath.
  Still live in me O loving strife
Of living Death and dying Life.
For while Thou sweetly slayest me,
Dead to myself I live in Thee.[27]
 —Richard Crashaw

God:
the bad people laghed at noah:
   "You [made] an ark on dry land, you fool."
But he was smart
He stuck with you,
thats what I would do.[28]

                        —Eddie (child)

Search me, O God search me and know my heart,
Try me and prove me in the hidden part;
Cleanse me and make me holy as Thou art,
And lead me in the way everlasting.

Give me the heart that naught can change or chill,
The love that loves unchanged through good or ill,
The joy that through all trials triumphs still,
And lead me in the way everlasting.

Take my poor heart and only let me love
The things that always shall abiding prove;
Bind all my heart-strings to the world above,
And lead me in the way everlasting.[29]

                        —A. B. Simpson

        Temper my intemperance, Lord,
        O hallowed, O adored,
        My heart's creator, mighty, wild,
        Temper Thy bewildered child.
        Blaze my eye and blast my ear,
        Let me never fear to fear
        Nor forget what I have heard,
        Even your voice, my Lord.
        Even your Word.[30]

                —Madeleine L'Engle

Pronounce me, gracious God, thy son;
Own me an heir divine;
I'll pity princes on the throne,
When I can call thee mine:
  Sceptres and crowns unenvied rise,
  And lose their lustre in mine eyes.[31]
                              —Anonymous,
                              Lincoln's Devotional

Must I be carried to the skies
On flowery beds of ease,
While others fought to win the prize,
And sailed through bloody seas?

Since I must fight if I would reign
Increase my courage, Lord;
I'll bear the toil, endure the pain,
Supported by Thy Word.[32]
                              —Isaac Watts

Into my heart, empty and waiting,
Over my soul, needy and still,
Through my whole being, consuming and purging,
Sweep Thou, until—
Thou shalt see through my eyes,
Think through my brain,
Love through my heart,
And speak through my lips.
All of my being merging in Thine,
Holy Spirit divine.
Now, filled with the source of all beauty and power
Renewed life is mine,
Flowing within me each day and hour
From the Divine.[33]
                              —Miriam Reed

Since the dear hour that brought me to Thy foot,
And cut up all my follies by the root,
I never trusted in an arm but Thine,
Nor hoped but in Thy righteousness divine—
Cast at Thy glorious feet, mine only plea
Is what it was: dependence upon Thee.[34]

—Anonymous,
Lincoln's Devotional

I knew Thee not, Thou wounded Son of God,
Till I with Thee the path of suffering trod;
Till in the valley, through the gloom of night,
I walked with Thee, and turned to Thee for light.

I did not know the mystery of love,
The love that doth the fruitless branch remove;
The love that spares not e'en the fruitful tree,
But prunes, that it may yet more fruitful be.

I did not know the meaning of the Cross;
I counted it but bitterness and loss,
Till in Thy gracious discipline of pain
I found the loss I dreaded purest gain.

And shall I cry, e'en on the darkest day,
"Lord of all mercy, take my cross away"?
Nay, in the Cross I saw Thine open face,
And found therein the fulness of Thy grace.[35]

—George Briggs

10

Prayers of and for Love and Kindness

God of opportunity,
I find that there are too many choices confronting me.
I must do my work,
make time for my family,
fulfill social obligations,
support my church,
and give my money—
My plate is too full!
I do not have the time or the energy
to do all the things that the Gospel calls me to do!
When is enough really enough?
On top of everything else
you confront me with the poor.
Their need never ceases.
Their presence is ever before me.
I do not know how to help someone
who is so different from me.
Why are they here?
I try to do my share; I am a good person.
Why should there be more opportunity to give to others

than there is desire to give?
I do not really want to involve myself with them,
but the call is quiet and persistent for me to do so.
Why did you cast your lot with the poor?
Why do you call me to do the same?
Understand, Lord, that I do not really want to,
but I will try.[1]

—Micheal Elliott

Our Father in Heaven, we read in the Bible that love does not insist on its own way. Help us to love that we may live according to this precept. So often we feel that ours is the only way of doing a particular thing. We think, in the imagination of our hearts, that no one has as good ideas or as acceptable a plan as we have. And we realize, as we survey the life about us, that such thinking is not only wrong but troublesome. How many homes have been broken and friendships separated because one or both parties insisted on being counted right? Grant that we may have hearts big enough to give credit to other people's thoughts and desires. Create within us sufficient love that we may honor our brother as we would like to be honored by him.[2]

—William Kadel

Lord, when my eye confronts my heart, and I realize that you have filled my heart with your love, I am breathless with amazement. Once my heart was so small in its vision, so narrow in its compassion, so weak in its zeal for truth. Then you chose to enter my heart, and now in my heart I can see you, I can love all your people, and I have courage to proclaim the truth of your gospel to anyone and everyone. Like wax before a fire, my heart has melted under the heat of your love.[3]

—Count Von Zinzendorf

Zinzendorf left his court position in Germany to become a spiritual leader with the Moravians. With the Halle Pietists, the Moravians launched the modern Protestant missions movement.

To all the humble beasts there be,
To all the birds on land and sea,
Great Spirit, sweet protection give
That free and happy they may live!
And to our hearts the rapture bring
Of love for every living thing;
Make us all one kin, and bless
Our ways with Christ's own gentleness.[4]
　　　　　　　　—John Galsworthy

Passionate Lord,
we "naturally," "understandably," "prudently,"
prefer the wisdom of the Buddha, who said,
"He who loves fifty has fifty woes, who loves none
  has no woe,"
for it hurts to care, to extend, to let other lives matter,
because they suffer, and they fail, and they die,
and we'd rather not hurt so;
But we are haunted by Your Holy Fool
who cried over Jerusalem and wept for Lazarus,
who feels each pain and every body's aches,
who suffered about, with, for all
and loves every soul as if it were his own child.
We have much to repent
more to learn, most to feel
for Christ's sake, amen.[5]
　　　　　　　　—Frederick Ohler

Give me the lowest place, not that I dare
Ask for that lowest place, but Thou hast died
That I might live and share
Thy glory by Thy side.

Give me the lowest place; or if for me
That lowest place too high, make one more low
Where I may sit and see
My God and love Thee so.[6]
　　　　　　　　—Christina Rossetti

Mighty God! Creator unbegun, unending!

Your works, when I think that they are yours, dazzle me to silence and to awe and aweful prayer. For I may know some little something of the sun. . . . But what do such solar figures do to the size of me? And what are my own travels and my age and my death beside this brutal fire in the universe? Tiny, tiny, insignificant. My God, the little that I know of your sun, and this but one among a sea of suns, belittles me. How is it that you love me?

Who can say . . . how first you bulged that sun into its place, and hammered its brazen face, and shocked it at the heart, and set it afire? Who knows the word wherewith you commanded the sun to be? We chirp theories like chickadees, because ignorance is a terrifying thing and we need the noise. But when I can with courage know I do not know; when I admit that I stand with my back to a void . . . then I am silenced. Then I am chilled by my own triviality—some dust at the edge of a desert. Nevertheless, you kneel down, and find me, and tell me that you love me.

And even as I am dust in space, so am I but an instant in time—always an instant: the end of the year that ended yesterday, the beginning of the year that begins today, the morning of that day, the minute, the second that ticks for me now. How insignificant, small, and pipping this moment! How like a rat's tooth, unworthy of any memory. Yet it is me.

You enter from the other side of time; you stride from timelessness to this sole moment, to the ragged stretch of my existence, to me, to love me. How can such a kindness be?

For you who made time are not bound by time—except you choose to be. You embrace me, my dribble of moments. Right now you are standing at my birth, receiving me an infant into this created world. Yet right now you are present for this prayer of mine, prayed between the years. Right now you are establishing the answers of our prayers in our futures, in your present. And right now, dear God, you are waiting at my death, your hands extended, ready to receive me to your kingdom—not only the same God that hears me now, but in the same eternal moment as now I pray!

You are wonderful beyond describing it. And still you choose to notice me. . . . You bend your boundless being, your infinity, into space and time, into things and into history, to find me, to preserve my life. How is it that you care for me?

I whisper, amazed that you should care to hear it. I whisper here, now, the truth of my heart and the wholeness of my being: I whisper, God, I love you, too.[7]

—Walter Wangerin (excerpted)

O my God, possess my soul with such an ardent love of Thee, so buoyant above all other affections, that no one may ever come in competition with it; such a love as may not only subdue all other affections, but purify and make them innocent; such a love as may create in my soul a perpetual pleasure in the contemplation of Thee, and a continual thirst after Thee; a love which may transport my soul with Thy divine perfections. And paint there such bright ideas of Thy glorious majesty that none of the trifling pleasures and temptations of this world may be able to make on it the least impression. And as, my gracious Lord, Thou hast given me much, and forgiven me much, so raise my love to a degree proportionable to Thy bounty and mercy.[8]

—Charles How

Though sorrows rise and dangers roll
In waves of darkness o'er my soul;
Though friends are false and love decays,
And few and evil are my days—
Yet e'en in nature's utmost ill,
I love thee, Lord! I love thee still.[9]

—Anonymous,
Lincoln's Devotional

O God, grant that all through today I may never find any request for help a nuisance. Let me never find a child a nuisance when he wants me to help him with his lessons or play with him in his games.

Help me never to find a sick person a nuisance, if she would like me to spend some time with her or do some service for her.

Help me never to find someone who is old a nuisance even if he is critical of youth, settled immovably in his ways, demanding of attention.

Help me never to find a nuisance anyone who asks me to show her how to do things, to assist her in her work, to listen to her troubles.

Grant, O God, that I may neither be too immersed in work or too fond of my own pleasure, that I may never be too busy and never too tired to help those who need help, even if they are the kind of people who get on my nerves or whom I instinctively dislike.

Help me to help, not only when it's pleasant to help, but when help is difficult and when I don't want to give it—through Jesus Christ my Lord.[10]

—William Barclay

I ask you, Lord Jesus,
　　to develop in me, your lover,
　　　　an immeasurable urge towards you,
　　　　an affection that is unbounded,
　　　　a longing that is unrestrained,
　　　　a fervour that throws discretion to the winds!
The more worthwhile our love for you,
　　all the more pressing does it become.
Reason cannot hold it in check,
　　fear does not make it tremble,
　　　　wise judgment does not temper it.[11]

—Richard Rolle

O Lord, grant that each one who has to do with me today may be the happier for it. Let it be given me each hour what I shall say, and grant me the wisdom of a loving heart that I may say the right thing rightly.

Help me to enter into the mind of everyone who talks with

me, and keep me alive to the feelings of each one present. Give me a quick eye for little kindnesses, that I may be ready in doing them and gracious in receiving them. Give me quick perception of the feelings and needs of others, and make me eager-hearted in helping them.[12]

—H. M. Soulsby

O Lord, who art full of love and mercy, help me to be careful of the feelings of others. Let me beware of the hasty word, the prying question, and the indelicate allusion that hurt worse than a blow. Show me how to put the shy at ease, and to give them confidence by words of kindness and true interest in them. Keep me from blundering into the sacred places of others. Give me a wholesome sense of the rights of others, that I may not even appear to disregard them. Bestow on me keen insight, that I may see at once the fitting thing to do.[13]

—E. Scovil

My dear Lord,
I depend wholly upon thee—wean me from all other dependences.
Thou art my all, thou dost overrule all and delight in me.
Thou art the foundation of goodness. . . .
      how can I distrust thee?
      how be anxious about what happens to me?
In the light of thy preciousness
      the world and all its enjoyments are infinitely poor:
I value the favor of men no more than pebbles.
Amid the blessings I receive from thee
may I never lose the heart of a stranger.
May I love thee, my benefactor, in all my benefits,
      not forgetting that my greatest danger arises from my
        advantages.
Produce in me self-despair that will make Jesus precious to me,
      delightful in all his offices,
      pleasureable in all his ways,
      and may I love his commands as well as his promises.

Help me to discern between true and false love,
        the one consisting of supreme love to thee, the other not,
        the former uniting thy glory and human happiness
        that they may become one common interest,
        the latter disjointing and separating them both,
        seeking the latter with neglect of the former.
Teach me that genuine love is different in kind
    from that wrought by rational arguments or the motive of
    self-interest,
    that such love is a pleasing passion affording joy to the mind
    where it is.
        Grant me grace to distinguish between the genuine and
        the false,
And to rest in thee who art all love.[14]

—Puritan Prayer

More love to Thee, O Christ,
More love to Thee.
Hear Thou the prayer I make
On bended knee;
This is my earnest plea—
More love, O Christ, to Thee,
More love to Thee.

Let sorrow do its work,
Send grief and pain;
Sweet are Thy messengers,
Sweet their refrain,
When they can sing with me,
More love, O Christ, to Thee,
More love to Thee.[15]

—E. P. Prentiss

Blessed Lord, we know so little of the love of the Father. Although this is one of the first, simplest, and most glorious lessons in your school, you know that it is one of the hardest to learn. Lord, teach us so to live with the Father that his love may be nearer, clearer, dearer to us than the love of any earthly father. And let the assurance of his hearing our prayer be as much greater than the confidence in an earthly parent as the heavens are higher than earth. To this extent, you are infinitely greater than humanity. Lord, show us that only our unchildlike distance from the Father hinders the answer to prayer. Lead us on to the true life of God's children. Lord Jesus, we see that it is fatherlike love that awakens childlike trust. Reveal the Father and his tender, pitying love to us that we may become childlike and experience that power of prayer that lies in the child-life.

Blessed Son of God, the Father loves you and has given you all things. And you love the Father, and have done all things He commanded you, and therefore you have the power to ask all things. Lord, give us your own Spirit, the Spirit of the Son. Make us childlike, as you were on earth. And let every prayer be breathed in the faith that as the heaven is higher than the earth, so your Father-love and your readiness to give us what we ask surpasses all we can think or conceive.[16]

—Andrew Murray

O God, help me all through today to do nothing to worry those who love me, to do nothing to let down those who trust me, to do nothing to fail those who employ me, to do nothing to hurt those who are close to me.

Help me all through this day to do nothing which would be a cause of temptation to someone else or which would make it easier for someone else to go wrong; not to discourage anyone who is doing his best; not to dampen anyone's enthusiasms or to increase anyone's doubts.

Let me all through this day be a comfort to the sad, be a friend to the lonely, be an encouragement to the dispirited, be a help to those who are up against it. So grant that others may see in me something of the reflection of the Master whose I am and whom I seek to serve.[17]

—William Barclay

Dear God,
I bet it is very hard
for you to love all of
everybody in the whole
world. There are only 4
people in our family and
I can never do it.[18]

         —Nan (child)

Lord Jesus Christ, today I want to live my life as an expression of your love rather than as an effort to earn or deserve your love. Like Paul, I have tried about everything to prove my worth. Nothing satisfies. I am weary of doing the right thing because of guilt and not grace. Thank you for the limitless power of your love which sets me free from a "guilted" cage to fly and soar to new heights of joyous praise today. Amen.[19]

         —Lloyd John Ogilvie

Lord, may we love all your creation, all the earth and every grain of sand in it. May we love every leaf, every ray of your light.

May we love the animals: you have given them the rudiments of thought and joy untroubled. Let us not trouble it; let us not harass them, let us not deprive them of their happiness, let us not work against your intent.

For we acknowledge unto you that all is like an ocean, all is flowing and blending, and that to withhold any measure of love from anything in your universe is to withhold that same measure from you.[20]

         —Fyodor Dostoevsky

Dear God, I just want someone to love me, someone to talk to when I need to talk. Someone to cry on when I need to cry. Most of all, someone to love me and walk as far as they wish through my life.

         —Anonymous teen

This teen was from Covenant House, a crisis center for homeless youth in New York.

> Glorious God, give me grace to amend my life, and to have an eye to my end without begrudging death, which to those who die in you, good Lord, is the gate of a wealthy life.
>
> And give me, good Lord, a humble, lowly, quiet, peaceable, patient, charitable, kind, tender and pitiful mind, in all my works and all my words and all my thoughts. . . .
>
> Give me, good Lord, a longing to be with you, not to avoid the calamities of this world, nor so much to attain the joys of heaven, as simply for love of you.
>
> And give me, good Lord, your love and favour, which my love of you, however great it might be, could not deserve were it not for your great goodness.[21]
>
> —Thomas More

More would not support King Henry VIII in his divorce, nor would he swear loyalty to Henry as head of the Church of England. He declared he was the king's servant, but God's first, and, for this, he was executed. This prayer was written a week before his death.

> May I feel beneath my wrongs
> Vengeance to the Lord belongs;
> Nor a worse requital dare,
> Than the sweet revenge of prayer:
> Much forgiven, may I learn,
> Love for hatred to return.[22]
>
> —Anonymous,
> *Lincoln's Devotional*

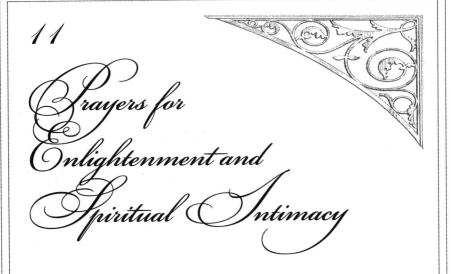

11

Prayers for Enlightenment and Spiritual Intimacy

'Mid all the traffic of the ways,
Turmoils without, within,
Make in my heart a quiet place,
And come and dwell therein:

A little shrine of quietness,
All sacred to Thyself,
Where Thou shalt all my soul possess,
And I may find myself:

A little shelter from life's stress,
Where I may lay me prone,
And bare my soul in loneliness,
and know as I am known:

A little place of mystic grace,
Of self and sin swept bare,
Where I may look upon Thy face,
And talk with Thee in prayer.[1]
—John Oxenham

This prayer was written in 1917 in a London chapel. There, the poet had gone to muse and pray upon receiving word that his son had been killed in action.

Dear God,
Do good people have to die young?
I heard my mommy say that. I am not
always good.[2]

Yours truly,
Barbara (child)

My God, I love Thee, not because
  I hope for heaven thereby,
Nor yet because who love Thee not
  Are lost eternally.

Thou, O my Jesus, Thou didst me
  Upon a cross embrace;
For me didst bear the nails and spear
  And manifold disgrace.

And griefs and torments numberless,
  And sweat of agony;
Yea, death itself—and all for me
  Who was thine enemy.

Then why, O blessed Jesus Christ,
  Should I not love thee well?
Not for the sake of winning heaven,
  Nor of escaping hell.

Not from the hope of gaining aught,
   Not seeking a reward;
But as Thyself hast loved me,
   O ever-loving Lord.

So would I love Thee, dearest Lord,
   And in Thy praise will sing;
Solely because Thou art my God,
   And my most loving King.[3]

          —Francis Xavier

Oh, I can hear you, God, above the cry
   Of the tossing trees—
Rolling your windy tides across the sky,
And splashing your silver seas
   Over the pine,
   To the water line
   Of the moon.
Oh, I can hear you, God,
Above the wail of the lonely loon—
When the pine-tops pitch and nod—
   Chanting your melodies
Of ghostly waterfalls and avalanches,
Washing your wind among the branches
To make them pure and white.
Wash over me, God, with your piney breeze,
   And your moon's wet-silver pool;
Wash over me, God, with your wind and night,
   And leave me clean and cool.[4]

          —Lew Sarett

I will not hurry through this day.
Lord, I will listen by the way,
To humming bees and singing birds,
To speaking trees and friendly words;
And for the moments in between
Seek glimpses of Thy great unseen.

I will not hurry through this day;
I will take time to think and pray;
I will look up into the sky,
Where fleecy clouds and swallows fly;
And somewhere in the day, maybe
I will catch whispers, Lord, from Thee.[5]
—Ralph Spalding Cushman

Jesus, Thou joy of loving hearts,
  Thou fount of life, Thou light of men,
From the best bliss that earth imparts
  We turn unfilled to Thee again.

Our restless spirits yearn for Thee,
  Where'er our changeful lot is cast—
Glad when Thy gracious smile we see,
  Blest when our faith can hold Thee fast.

O Jesus, ever with us stay;
  Make all our moments calm and bright;
Chase the dark night of sin away,
  Shed o'er the world Thy holy light.[6]
—Bernard of Clairvaux

As pants the hart for cooling streams,
  When heated in the chase;
So longs my soul, O God, for thee,
  And Thy refreshing grace.

For Thee, my God, the living God,
  My thirsty soul doth pine;
Oh, when shall I behold Thy face,
  Thou Majesty divine?

God of my strength, how long shall I,
  Like one forgotten, mourn;

Forlorn, forsaken, and exposed
To my oppressor's scorn?

Why restless, why cast down, my soul?
Trust God; who will employ
His aid for thee, and change these sighs
To thankful hymns of joy.[7]
—Nahum Tate

I hate the thick darkness
that swells and swells inside of me
When I am alone.

Am I alone, God?
I feel like a shriveled hand clutching at the air;
Like a torn arm twisting in the sand . . .
I am choking, God, in my own sour thoughts.
I keep dredging them from the past
As though they were important;
They blind my brain like clots of blood . . .
All I ask is one person, God—
One ear that will not close
no matter what I say;
One hand that will not make
me choke or draw away;
One heart that will not turn me off
no matter how I act.[8]
—Candy (adolescent)

Speak, Lord, in the stillness,
While I wait on Thee;
Hushed my heart to listen
In expectancy.

Speak, O blessed Master,
In this quiet hour;

Let me see Thy face, Lord,
Feel Thy touch of power.

For the words Thou speakest,
They are life, indeed;
Living bread from heaven,
Now my spirit feed.

Speak, Thy servant heareth,
Be not silent, Lord;
Waits my soul upon Thee
For the quickening word.[9]
—E. May Grimes

Lord, as we observe how the innermost character of nature is revealed in growth—how even rocks and crystals grow—rid us of complacency, of all pride in our attainments which can be but ordinary, even at their best. May we be filled with a divine discontent that shall make the wise seek to be wiser, the pure, purer, the strong, stronger. May we do every piece of work more perfectly; may we love more deeply, attack evil more boldly.

Especially give us genuine contact with Jesus Christ. May we not be satisfied with borrowed opinions about Him or scholarly expositions of His life or eloquent sermons that laud Him, but help us to know Him and the fellowship of His cross and the power of His resurrection through the ordeal of personal and pursuing inquiry, sharp self-discipline, and brave obedience to His commands. In His light help us to see everything as it is: the true as true, the false as false.[10]
—Frederick Lewis

How long it's been since You and I
meandered down the garden path,
in muted conversation dared
to name the wonders that we shared.

What think you of the stars, my child?
What wags the puppy's tail, my Lord?
Your stainless angels gently spread
white roses on the path ahead.

Yet I would trade, and have indeed,
that unpicked paradise we knew
to spend today beside your Son
who walks among what choice has spun.

His word describes not joy decreed
but consecrates the jumbled now,
assuring us of liberty,
the essence of our dignity.

If all was lost, now all is gain
for children thrust from Eden's gate
who grow apace amid the strife;
the chosen choose your Christ, the life.[11]
—Roger Swenson

Abide with me, fast falls the eventide;
The darkness deepens, Lord, with me abide;
When other helpers fail, and comforts flee,
Help of the helpless, O abide with me.

Hold thou thy Cross before my closing eyes;
Shine through the gloom, and point me to the skies;
Heaven's morning breaks, and earth's vain shadows flee,
In life, in death, O Lord, abide with me.[12]
—William Bright

If we have never sought, we seek Thee now;
Thine eyes burn through the dark, our only stars;
We must have sight of thorn-pricks on Thy brow,
We must have Thee, O Jesus of the Scars.

The heavens frighten us, they are too calm;
   In all the universe we have no place.
Our wounds are hurting us, where is thy balm?
   Lord Jesus, by Thy scars we claim Thy grace.

If when the doors are shut, Thou drawest near,
   Only reveal those hands, that side of Thine;
We know today what wounds are, have no fear,
   Show us Thy scars, we know the countersign.

The other gods were strong, but Thou wast weak,
   They rode, but Thou didst stumble to a throne;
But to our wounds God's wounds alone can speak,
   And not a god has wounds, but Thou alone.[13]
                    —Edward Shillito

Lord, do you know what it's like to be a clown? Do you know what it's like for a girl to be born a circus act? Do you know what it's like to have a funny bone for a brain? I have a smile that's . . . always there, and everyone expects it to be there. . . . I can't enjoy a bad mood with other people. That's a strange luxury. I have to be a clown—whenever people tease me, I turn into an act . . . , a fool standing on my head. Then I look up and see a world full of upside down people trying to be what they aren't.

   I'm waiting for someone to step behind my face and find me. Not just Stevie, but me, Lord. When will I be free to be me? I cry real tears just like them.[14]
                    —Stevie (adolescent; adapted)

Dear God,

   I've seen you several times these last days, sometimes in the most unsuspecting places and sometimes just the evidence that you have been there—through your footprints.

   Without her really knowing it, I think it was your Spirit in our Russian friend that caused her to send a special little Christmas gift over to each one of us.

And the other morning when I came down to breakfast, I knew you had been there in the spirit of my granddaughter, who, before she went to school, left a little note on my plate. . . . It read, "I love you, Grandma, very much."

Yes, and you must have been the one that caused Karl, our grandson, after he had finished his three days of entrance exams, to say to me, "Grandma, would it help if I typed your letters for you?"

When it snowed the other night . . . I saw you in Biz, shoveling off the walk of the lonely widow across the street.

And it was you in the heart of that young Indonesian pastor prompting him to leave his family in Munich and come to Stuttgart to help the wife and family of his friend who was having an operation.

I saw you in those spectacular amaryllis, that breathtaking bouquet that Biz's friend sent to visibly bring your presence into this house.

I heard you last night, Lord, in that glorious concert in the Stifts Kirche, when soloists, choir, and instruments combined to interpret the gifts of music you gave to Bach, Mozart, and Beethoven.

I heard you in your Word this morning as I read about the daring of your apostles as they witnessed to your life and resurrection. I heard you and was ashamed of my own cowardice. . . .

You were in the sensitive kindness of that young man who changed his plans for the evening to accompany that weird and bewildered old man to dinner and to make the occasion a happy one.

How many times do I miss your footprints in the course of a day? I'm so quick to see the wrong and the ugly in people. Please open my eyes to your presence. . . . And work a miracle again, Lord. Let people see you in me![15]

—Ruth Youngdahl Nelson
(excerpted)

Ruth Nelson was voted Mother of the Year in 1973.

Jesus, I come to you, overcome with revulsion
by the spittle on your face. . . .
It slides down your cheeks,
it comes in the corner of your eye,
it sickens me, that sight.

I cry out in that ugliness.
I come to you, Jesus, with cloth and water
to wipe away degradation,
to wash away the filth thrown from the bystanders.

You lower your head to my hand
and the slime comes on the cloth,
it hardly washes in water, so thick is it upon your face.
The touch of human defilement clings to the creases of your
    cheek.

I have felt this painful deed
as I, too, have known rejection,
have heard, and hurt, with words
thrown like spittle in my face.

I have felt marred and maimed in spirit
as my very person was cruelly rebuffed.
I have felt the slime and contempt
stick and press upon my life.

The recognition of my own pain and derision
almost overpowers my sad soul;
I stand stunned and sorrowful inside myself.
I want to comfort you, Jesus;
I want to be comforted by you.

Jesus, spat upon and rejected,
have mercy on us all.[16]

—Joyce Rupp

Jesus, lover of my soul, let me to thy bosom fly,
while the waters nearer roll, while the tempest still is high,
hide me, O my Savior, hide, till the storm of life is past;
safe into the haven glide. O receive my soul at last.[17]

—Charles Wesley

Thyself, O my God, thyself for thine own sake, above all things else I love. Thyself I desire. Thyself as my last end I long for. Thyself for thine own sake, not anything else whatsoever, always and in all things I seek, with all my heart and marrow, with groaning and weeping, with unbroken toil and grief.

What wilt Thou render me therefore for my latter end? If Thou render me not thyself, Thou givest nothing. If I find not thyself, I find nothing. To no purpose Thou rewardest me, but dost wrong me sore. For, if ever I sought Thee, I hoped to find Thee at the last and to keep Thee. And with this honeyed hope in all my toils was I sweetly comforted. But now, if Thou have denied me thyself, whatever else you give me, if you frustrate so high a hope, not for a little time but forever, shall I not languish with love, mourn with grief, weep for the fact that I shall always exist empty and void. Shall I not sorrow inconsolably, complain unceasingly, be wrung unendingly?

This is not thy property, O best, most gracious, most loving God; in no way is it congruous. Make me therefore, O best my God, in the life present always to love thyself for thyself before all things, to seek Thee in all things, and at the last in the life to come to find and to keep Thee forever.[18]

—Lancelot Andrewes
(edited for clarity)

In the quiet of the early morning, Lord,
I bring my thoughts to you.
   I turn off the radio
and I am quiet inside.
   I concentrate
on what you have spoken to me.
   Then I allow you

to walk into my soul,
   to lift me up,
to move where the real me lives.
   I feel myself awake,
not to the problems
   of the coming day,
but to you.
   I feel at one with you, Lord.
I feel your love and concern,
   and it's what I love to feel.
I love the safety and peace
   that comes into me when I know
the day is in your hands.
   I pray I can be an expression
of what you have given me.[19]

       —Jill (adolescent)

Lord, give me courage and love to open the door and constrain You to enter, whatever the disguise You come in, even before I fully recognize my guest.

Come in! Enter my small life!

Lay Your sacred hands on all the common things and small interests of that life and bless and change them. Transfigure my small resources, make them sacred. And in them give me Your very Self.[20]

       —Evelyn Underhill

It's not that I'm unattractive, Lord,
I'm ugly.
It's very lonely loving myself tonight.
I feel so empty and torn
between my white sheets.
I sense the smiles and faces
and hands of other kids
but they're not meant for me, not really.

I try to reach out
and touch my friends.
I want to find the feel of love . . .
I want my nerves to quiver
with the excitement of love.
I dream about the brush
of skin on skin
of soul with soul . . .
But dreams are only lonely thoughts . . .
Were you lonely, Lord?
Were you lonely on the cross
without your clothes
and your friends?
Were you lonely
asleep in that cold tomb
for two long silent nights?

Help me to love
as you loved,
without being empty
and lonely
and torn.[21]

—Sandra (age 15)

Give me, Lord Jesu, this special grace, to rest me in Thee above all creatures; above all health and fairness, above all glory and honor, above all dignity and power, above all cunning and policy, above all riches and crafts, above all gladness of body and soul, above all fame and praising, above all sweetness and consolation, above all hope and promise, above all merit and desire; above all gifts and rewards that Thou mayest give or send beside Thyself, and above all joy and mirth that man's heart or mind may take or feel. Also above all angels and archangels, and above the company of heavenly spirits, above all things visible and invisible. . . .

Thou, O Lord God, art the best, most high, most mighty, most comfortable, most fair, most loving, most noble, and most glorious above all things; in whom all goodness together perfectly and fully is, hath been, and shall be. And therefore, whatsoever Thou givest me beside Thyself, it is little and insufficient to me for my heart may not rest nor fully be pacified but in Thee, so that it ascendeth above all gifts, and also above all things that be created.

O Jesu, the light and brightness of everlasting glory, the joy and comfort of all Christian people that are walking and laboring in the wilderness of this world, my heart crieth to Thee by still desires without voice and my silence speaketh unto Thee. . . . Come, Lord, come for without Thee I have no glad day nor hour; for Thou art all my joy and without Thee my soul is barren and void. I will not cease of prayer till Thy grace return to me again, and Thou speak inwardly to my soul and say thus: "Lo, I am here. I am come to thee, for thou hast called Me. Thy tears and the desire of thy heart, thy meekness and thy contrition have bowed me down and brought Me to thee."

There is none like to Thee, Lord, in heaven or in earth. Thy works be good. Thy judgments be righteous, and by Thy providence all things be governed. Wherefore to Thee, who art the Wisdom of the Father, be everlasting joy and glory. And I humbly beseech Thee, that my body and soul, my heart and tongue, and all Thy creatures, may ever laud Thee and bless Thee.[22]

—Thomas à Kempis

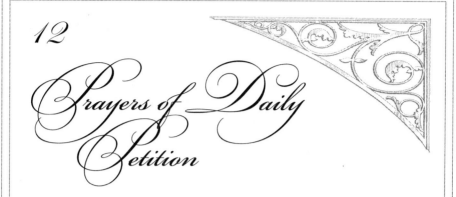

12

Prayers of Daily Petition

Give us, Lord, a bit o' sun,
A bit o' work and a bit o' fun;
Give us all in the struggle and sputter
Our daily bread and a bit o' butter;
Give us health, our keep to make,
An' a bit to spare for others' sake.
Give us sense, for we're some of us duffers,
An' a heart to feel for all that suffers;
Give us, too, a bit of a song
And a tale and a book to help us along.
An' give us our share o' sorrow's lesson
That we may prove how grief's a blessin'.
Give us, Lord, a chance to be
Our goodly best, brave, wise, and free,
Our goodly best for yourself and others
Till all men learn to live as brothers.[1]

— Found on the wall of an old inn,
Lancaster, England

Dear God (God of Justice),

I hate to bother you but there's this kid. His name is Billy Forte. He's always bothering me and being mean. He tried to steal my glove.

Can you rub him out? Sorry to bug you.[2]

—John [age 8]

O thou Chief of Chiefs, we kneel before thee in obeisance and adoration. Like the village sharpening-stone, thou art always available and never exhausted. Remove, we pray thee, our sins that hide thy face. Thou knowest that we are poor and un-learned; that we often work when hungry. Send rain in due season for our gardens that our food may not fail. Protect us from the cold and danger by night. Help us to keep in health that we may rejoice in strength. May our villages be filled with children. Emancipate us from the fear of the fetish and the witch doctor and from all manner of superstitions. Save the people, especially the Christian boys and girls in the villages, from the evil that surrounds them. All this we ask in the name of Jesus Christ thy Son.[3]

—A prayer from Zaire, Africa

Dear Lord,

Do you have any favorite Christians? I would like to be one.[4]

—Mary [age 8]

O God, thou art with me and it is thy will that these outward tasks are given me to do. Therefore I ask thee, assist me, and through it all let me continue in thy presence. Be with me in this my endeavor, accept the labor of my hands, fill my heart as always.[5]

—Brother Lawrence,
France, seventeenth century

Dear father God,

Thank you for the gift of nature. For trees, flowers, fish, birds, and animals.

But, God, let us think about extinc creatures like the Great
Auk, the Pliosaur,
the Dodo, and the Passenger Pigeon.
And let us think about endagered species like the Tiger, the
Giant Panda, the
Golden Eagle, and the Elephant.
Oh God, please stop man destroying the home you made
for us.
Amen.[6]

—Toby Keeley (child)

I asked You, God, for strength that I might achieve;
I was made weak that I might learn to obey.
I asked for health that I might do greater things;
I was given infirmity that I might do better things.
I asked for riches that I might be happy;
I was given poverty that I might be wise.
I asked for power that I might have the praise of men;
I was given weakness that I might feel the need for You.
I asked for all things that I might enjoy life;
I was given *life* that I might enjoy all things.
I received nothing that I asked for, but all that I hoped for. . . .
My prayers were answered.[7]

—Prayer of an unknown
Confederate soldier
(personalized)

Our Father who is in heaven,
and here on earth too,
waiting to be heard,
waiting to be seen,
as we say the words
and go through the motions we have learned—
break through to us somehow.
We are too busy praying
to really communicate with you.
Our prayers are monologues

and not dialogues.
I have too much I want to say
so that I do not take the time to hear
what you want to say to me.
I do not sense your presence
when it passes by me.

I thank you for these times
and desire they happen more often,
but right now I am in a hurry.
I have to attend another banquet—
I have been asked to say grace.[8]
> —Micheal Elliott

Dear God,
Thank you for the baby brother
but what I prayed for was a puppy.[9]
> —Joyce (child)

Lord, I cannot let Thee go,
Till a blessing Thou bestow;
Do not turn away Thy face,
Mine's an urgent pressing case.
Dost Thou ask me who I am?
Ah, my Lord, Thou know'st my name;
Yet the question gives a plea
To support my suit with Thee.

Thou didst once a wretch behold,
In rebellion blindly bold,
Scorn Thy grace, Thy power defy;
That poor rebel, Lord, was I.
Once a sinner near despair
Sought Thy mercy-seat by prayer;
Mercy heard and set him free;
Lord, that mercy came to me.

Many days have pass'd since then,
Many changes I have seen;
Yet have been upheld till now;
Who could hold me up but Thou?
Thou hast help'd in every need,
This emboldens me to plead;
After so much mercy past,
Canst Thou let me sink at last?
No—I must maintain my hold,
'Tis Thy goodness makes me bold;
I can no denial take,
When I plead for Jesus' sake.[10]

     —John Newton

Give me a good digestion, Lord,
And also something to digest;
Give me a healthy body, Lord,
With sense to keep it at its best.
Give me a healthy mind, good Lord,
To keep the good and pure in sight,
Which seeing sin is not appalled
But finds a way to set it right.
Give me a mind that is not bored,
That does not whimper, whine, or sigh;
Don't let me worry overmuch
About the fussy thing called I.
Give me a sense of humor, Lord,
Give me the grace to see a joke,
To get some happiness from life
And pass it on to other folk.[11]

    —Found in Chester Cathedral,
         England

O God, why am I sometimes so concerned
with the amount of good works
more than I am with the work itself?
Why am I preoccupied with numbers
rather than the joy of helping?
Why do I define success in numerical terms
rather than with a spiritual definition?
I notice, Lord,
too many of your followers
count your sheep.
If they are so busy counting them,
when do they feed them?
Numbers can mislead, Lord.
A lot means I am doing good.
A few means I have fallen short.
Numbers can also intimidate, Lord.
When I look at the mass of poor and needy people,
people who need me,
I despair because there are too many.
Numbers can confuse me too, Lord.
You walk away from ninety-nine,
but I concede the loss and tend what is left.
Help me learn to count, Lord,
as you do.[12]

—Micheal Elliott

Loving God, here I am again, wanting answers, results, and quick fixes. I keep running but getting nowhere. Help me to slow down. Help me take the time to breathe in the reality of your presence in my life. Help me to listen and, most of all, really hear what you are saying to me. When I only admit that all it takes is openness to you, all my inadequacies do fade away. I can take time to smell the roses and, at the same time, have all the strength and energy I so desperately seek. When I hear what you are saying, I can concentrate on the tasks that lie before me.

God of all life, I ask for your continuing patience with me—

I do so desperately need it. Grant the serenity that comes from hearing what you are saying and the life that comes when I finally respond to your word. I ask all this in the name of Jesus the Christ.[13]

—Martha Stoneburner

Dear God, Please put a-nother Holiday between Christmas and Easter. There is nothing good in there now.[14]

—Ginny (child)

I feel hurt, Lord. . . . She doesn't meet me in the park anymore . . . because she's in love with some other guy or she thinks she is. Well, he can have her for all I care. . . . Once it was a thrill to talk to her, to touch her. . . . We made promises to each other, secret promises. But she broke them. . . .

I wish he were dead. . . . He made me look like a little kid instead of a man. . . . Do you know how I feel? I pretend I'm not hurt. I can't tell the other guys—they'd laugh at me. Everyone likes to laugh as long as it's not their head that's being chopped off. . . . Dad laughed when I told him. . . . Help me, Lord, before I'm too old and too broken to love again the way I loved Mary.[15]

—Tim (adolescent)

Our Father which art in heaven, Hallowed be thy name. Thy kingdom come. Thy will be done in earth, as it is in heaven. Give us this day our daily bread. And forgive us our debts, as we forgive our debtors. And lead us not into temptation, but deliver us from evil: For thine is the kingdom, and the power, and the glory, for ever. Amen.

—Jesus Christ
Matthew 6:9–13 KJV

Our Father—*for we belong to Thee, however cut off from the rest of Thy family we may be. . . .*
Hallowed by Thy name—*nothing is hallowed here.*

Thy kingdom come—*already we have spent two years
here for Thee with few signs of a break. . . .*
Give us this day our daily bread—*we are out of eggs and
vegetables and there are no shops. . . .*
And forgive us our trespasses—*conditions seem sometimes to bring the worst out of us. . . .*
Deliver us from evil—*rumors of Nosu killings. . . .*
For Thine is the Kingdom, and the power, and the
glory—*come quickly, Lord, and reign.*[16]

          —A. J. Broomhall

Broomhall, Hudson Taylor's nephew, lifted up this prayer during a
depressing period when he served as missionary among a remote
people group called the Nosu.

Lord, I need patches on my faith.
The cloth of courage has worn thin.
The threads of joy have been cut.
The pattern of right and wrong has faded out.
I don't pray for more love but for strength
To move the love I already have.
I don't pray for a new conscience but for sense
Enough to scrape the barnacles off the old one.
I don't pray to be commander in chief over my life
But a trustworthy private on a worthwhile mission.
I don't pray for a medal but for loyalty in my heart.[17]

         —Jeanette Struchen

Dear God,
Thanks for the memories.
I realize that it is now too late
to become a guard for the
Celtics, but there are other
things I want to do. . . .
Like winning a Pulitzer prize,
for example. How about
some help?[18]

         —David (child)

Lord, Thou knowest better than I know myself that I am growing older. . . . Keep my mind free from the recital of endless
details. Give me wings to get to the point. Seal my lips on my
aches and pains. They are increasing and love of rehearsing
them is becoming sweeter as the time goes by. I dare not ask
for grace enough to enjoy the tales of others' pains, but help
me to endure them with patience.

I also dare not ask for improved memory but for a growing
humility and a lessening cocksureness when my memory seems
to clash with the memories of others. Teach me the glorious
lesson that occasionally I may be mistaken. . . .

Give me the ability to see good things in unexpected places
and talents in unexpected people. And give me, O Lord, the
grace to tell them so.

Keep me from the fatal habit of thinking I must say something on every subject and on every occasion. Release me from
craving to straighten out everybody's affairs. Make me thought-
ful but not moody—helpful but not bossy. With my vast store
of wisdom, it seems a pity not to use it all. But Thou knowest,
Lord, that I want a few friends at the end.[19]

—A seventeenth century nun
(excerpted)

Be off, Satan, from this door and from these four walls. This
is no place for you; there is nothing for you to do here. This is
the place for Peter and Paul and the holy gospel; and this
is where I mean to sleep, now that my worship is done, in the
name of the Father and of the Holy Spirit.[20]

—One of the earliest
Christian prayers recorded

Dear God, when is the best time I can talk with you?
I know you are always listening, but when will you
be listening especially hard in Ann Arbor, Michigan?[21]

Sincerely yours,
Allen (child)

Lord God,
I pretend to know all about sex
because my friends expect me to know
and because I look like a woman . . .
I pretend to know, Lord,
but I'm scared. . . .
Sex is always there,
like a beautiful leopard
crouching inside of me. . . .
I feel excited when I wear a slim dress
and my hair shines. . . .
I feel like flying
when a boyfriend kisses me gently. . . .
Sex seems to be everywhere . . .
and it's always there in me
like a leopard—
a beautiful, dangerous leopard. . . .
God, you made me this way.
Please give me the power
to handle the powers inside me.
Is love that power?
Give me the strength to love
without being swallowed
by sex. . . .
Accept me, as I am, Lord.
Please love me,
now.[22]

—Michelle [age 16]

O God, life has taken a good deal from me, but I want to begin by thanking you for all that life has left me. I can see and read. I can hear and listen. I can talk with my friends. Though my body must stay in one place, I can still send my mind and my imagination in adventurous travel. Once I was too busy doing things to think. Now I can think until I reach you and the things which really matter.

I still have books I can read, music I can listen to, radio and

television, even games I can play in bed. In spite of all that, O God, I need your help more than I need anything else. Keep me cheerful even when it is very difficult. Keep me content when my whole being naturally wants to be resentful. Let me not become querulous, complaining, demanding. Keep me from self-pity. Help me to be truly grateful for all that is done for me; and, even when it's the last thing I feel like doing, help me to smile.

Bless the doctors and nurses and others who care for me, and give them skill to find a cure some day even for people like me. When I feel that I'm useless and a burden to others, help me to remember that I can still pray, and so help me constantly to uphold the hands of those I love and constantly to bear them and myself to your throne of grace.

All this I ask for your love's sake.[23]

—William Barclay
(for the bedridden)

Watch, dear Lord,
with those who wake, or watch, or weep tonight,
and give your angels charge over those who sleep.
Tend your sick ones, O Lord Christ,
rest your weary ones.
Bless your dying ones.
Soothe your suffering ones.
Pity your afflicted ones.
Shield your joyous ones.
And all for your love's sake,
Amen.[24]

—Augustine of Hippo

God, Please send me [a] pony.
I never ask for anything before.
You can look it up.[25]

—Bruce (child)

Almighty God, we respond to Thee in many different ways. Some deny Thee altogether. Others acknowledge Thee but ignore Thee.

Some take Thee seriously. Others tip the hat to Thee occasionally.

Some worship and adore Thee. Others could not care less. Some love Thee, others fear Thee.

Some know Thee. Others feel Thou art beyond knowing.

Some see Thee as a living reality; others as an impersonal force.

But whatever our attitude, Father in heaven, rarely do we think of Thee as practical or relevant to our personal or corporate problems. Help us understand that Thou art a God who cares—who seeks us—who longs for us. Help us see that Thou art the source of all wisdom and power—that Thou art an infinite resource available to meet our needs.

Forgive our indifference and grant us grace to call upon Thee however great or small our problems. Help us see in the cross the measure of Your love, Your nearness, Your availability. In the name of Him whose mission was that of a sacrificial servant.[26]

—Richard Halverson, Chaplain
United States Senate

Lord, who on earth didst minister
    To those who helpless lay
In pain and weakness, hear me now,
    As unto Thee I pray.
Give to mine eyes the power to see
    The hidden source of ill,
Give to my hand the healing touch
    The throb of pain to still.
Grant that mine ears be swift to hear
    The cry of those in pain;
Give to my tongue the words that bring
    Comfort and strength again.

Fill Thou my heart with tenderness,
 My brain with wisdom true
And when in weariness I sink,
 Strengthen Thou me anew.
So in Thy footsteps may I tread
 Strong in Thy strength always.
So may I do Thy blessed work
 And praise Thee day by day.[27]
     —Anonymous
    ("Physician's Prayer")

You have shown great kindness to your servant, my father David, because he was faithful to you and righteous and upright in heart. You have continued this great kindness to him and have given him a son to sit on his throne this very day.

Now, O Lord my God, you have made your servant king in place of my father David. But I am only a little child and do not know how to carry out my duties. Your servant is here among the people you have chosen, a great people, too numerous to count or number. So give your servant a discerning heart to govern your people and to distinguish between right and wrong. For who is able to govern this great people of yours?
      —Solomon
     1 Kings 3:6–9 NIV

Solomon spoke this prayer after he was crowned king. God rewarded Solomon, not only with wisdom but also with prosperity, peace, and long life.

O God Creator—who spills the firmament into my cup
And trails the stardust through the skies,
Who spreads the rainbow 'mid the rain
And beats the thunder 'gainst the earth,
Who shakes the clouds until they leak
And sprinkles dew down tiny blades,
Who splashes lightning o'er the hills
And squeezes sunbeams through the fog,

Who hides the buds in secret places
And beckons seasons to come forth,
Who strikes the hours of night and day
And counts the eggs within a nest,
Who plants the coral 'neath the sea
And strikes aflame some sleeping crater,
Who guides the seeds for human life
And leads the dying through the valley,
Who lifts the waves upon the seas
And spins the years into eternity—
Touch me again and make my life a miracle.[28]
                              —Jeanette Struchen

Reveal Thy presence now, O Lord,
    As in the Upper Room of old;
Break Thou our bread, grace Thou our board,
    And keep our hearts from growing cold.[29]
                              —Thomas Tiplady

Open unto me—light for my darkness.
Open unto me—courage for my fear.
Open unto me—hope for my despair.
Open unto me—peace for my turmoil.
Open unto me—joy for my sorrow.
Open unto me—strength for my weakness.
Open unto me—wisdom for my confusion.
Open unto me—forgiveness for my sins.
Open unto me—tenderness for my toughness.
Open unto me—love for my hates.
Open unto me—Thy Self for my self.

Lord, Lord, open unto me!
Amen.[30]

                              —Howard Thurman

Lord, sometimes I think
I can't strike another typewriter key.
I can't write another paragraph or word.
I can't even put a period
At the end of a sentence.
I look at the fat bundle
Of unanswered letters
And it all seems so futile
And time-consuming, so unending.
I can't think or concentrate.
What I write seems empty, lifeless.
I struggle to keep my thoughts coherent.
Yet, I know I must keep on.
I have committed myself
To a ministry of writing—
Writing letters!

And often, God, when I begin to question
My personal commitment
You send me a ray of hope . . .
A personal rainbow.
Someone stops me to say
    "Ten years ago, when I needed it most
    You sent me a letter of encouragement.
    I've read it a hundred times.
    It's worn and tear-stained
    But I'll treasure it forever."
Lord, I don't even remember writing.
It's been so long. . . .
But first, Lord
I must put a period after the sentence
I so wearily wrote just an hour ago.[31]
                              —Ruth Harms Calkin

I do not ask for mighty words
To leave the crowd impressed,
But grant my life may ring so true
My neighbor shall be blessed.

I do not ask for influence
To sway the multitude;
Give me a "word in season" for
the soul in solitude.

I ask no place of prominence
Where all the world can see,
But in some needy corner, Lord,
There let me work for Thee.[32]

—Barbara Ryberg

O LORD, God of my master Abraham, give me success today, and show kindness to my master Abraham. See, I am standing beside this spring, and the daughters of the townspeople are coming out to draw water. May it be that when I say to a girl, "Please let down your jar that I may have a drink," and she says, "Drink, and I'll water your camels too"—let her be the one you have chosen for your servant Isaac. By this I will know that you have shown kindness to my master.

—Unnamed servant
Genesis 24:12–14 NIV

This servant was sent by Abraham to find a suitable wife for his son Isaac.

Dear God, my name is Robert.
I want a baby brother. My mother
said to ask my father. My father said
to ask you. Do you think you can do it?
Good luck.[33]

—Robert (child)

13
Prayers of Intercession

Dear Lord,

Please help the sick get well, like my best friend who has a birth defect and my friend's mom who has M.S. Help those who don't know how to draw closer to you. Help missionaries around the world be comforted by your love in a land where they are the only known Americans and sometimes the only known Christians—like my friend in India.[1]

—Emily (age 13)

Lord help me live from day to day
In such a self-forgetful way,
That even when I kneel to pray,
My prayer shall be for—others.[2]

—Charles Meigs

Oh, this people have sinned a great sin, and have made them gods of gold. Yet now, if thou wilt forgive their sin—; and if not, blot me, I pray thee, out of thy book which thou hast written.

—Moses
Exodus 32:31–32 KJV

May the road rise to meet you,
may the wind be always at your back,
may the sun shine warm on your face,
the rain fall softly on your fields;
and until we meet again,
may God hold you in the palm of his hand.[3]

—Anonymous
(A Gaelic blessing)

On this [multiple] anniversary of Watergate, when we are being reminded of the arrogance of power and the deceit of trusted leadership, the epitaph of Uzziah, king of Judah, seems profoundly relevant: *As his power increased, his heart grew proud and this was his ruin* [2 Chron. 26:16, Jerusalem Bible].

Father in heaven, at a time when cynicism and distrust are epidemic, send us spiritual and moral renewal, and let it begin with leadership. Humble us, Lord, before it is too late. Restore us to the dream of our forefathers, and forbid that we should be willing to settle for anything less.[4]

—Richard Halverson, Chaplain
United States Senate

Lord, the wind and sea obey thee,
Moon and stars their homage pay thee;
Listen to us, as we pray thee,
Who on thee for all depend.

Bless all travellers and strangers,
Safely keep the ocean rangers,
Guide them in the midst of dangers,
All to thee we now commend.

Bless the friends we've left behind us;
Closer may our parting bind us,
May they dearer, better, find us,
When we reach our journey's end.

On our way, dear Lord, direct us,
Where we err do thou correct us;
From the powers of ill protect us,
From all perils us defend.

May we know thy presence o'er us,
See thy guiding hand before us,
Till thou safely dost restore us,
Love to love and friend to friend.

Holy God, in mercy bending,
Human souls with love befriending,
Fit us all for joy unending,
When this earthly course doth end.[5]

—P. D.

God, bless fathers, all fathers old and young.
Bless the new father holding his son or daughter in
    his arms for the first time.
(Steady his trembling, Lord, make his arms strong.)
Give him the ambition and strength to provide for its
    physical needs.
But even more, give him the love and common sense
    to provide for its
hungering heart.
Give him the time and the will to be its friend.
Give him wisdom, give him patience, give him justice
    in discipline.
Make him a hero in his youngster's eyes,
So that the word *Father* will always mean a person to
    be respected,
a fair and mighty man.

And God bless older fathers too.
Fathers who are weary from working for their young.
Fathers who are sometimes disappointed, discouraged.
Fathers whose children don't always turn out the way
    they'd hoped;

fathers of children who seem thoughtless, ungrateful,
    critical,
children who rebel.
Bless those fathers, Lord; comfort them.
And stay close to all these fathers when they must tell
    sons and daughters
goodbye,
when kids leave home, going off to college, or to marry,
    or to war—
fathers need to be steadied in their trembling then too,
    Lord.
(Mothers aren't the only ones who cry.)
Thou, our heavenly Father, must surely understand
    these earthly
fathers well.
We so often disappoint You, rebel against You, fail to
    thank You,
turn away from You.
So, in your infinite love (and infinite experience) bless
    fathers,
all fathers old and young.[6]

—Marjorie Holmes

> The Lord bless you and keep you;
> The Lord make His face to shine upon you,
> And be gracious unto you.
> The Lord lift up His countenance upon you,
> And give you peace
> Through Jesus Christ our Lord.[7]
>
> —*The Book of Common Prayer*

> O God, Thy heavens, in the hush of night,
> So awesome, with their galaxies alight,
> Stir to their depths our silent, brooding souls,
> As, all above, the wondrous scroll unrolls.

In tones more awesome than the scene we scan,
Thy voice bespeaketh in the heart of man,
A way of life comporting with Thine own,
Who hast not left us in the dark alone.

But Who, throughout our tragic night, art nigh,
In deep compassion ever standing by,
Until awakened, we shall see Thy face,
Thou Lover of our sadly stricken race.

O Living Spirit, all our powers reclaim;
Let Thy compassion set our souls aflame.
Form Thou in us a purpose true and pure,
That what we build together may endure.

High on the mountain of Thy holiness
Above the fogs, where Thou canst own and bless,
Help us the City of our God to build
Where all Thy plan for us may be fulfilled.

Then hither from the shadows yet shall throng
The multitudes unblest to join the song
Whose joyous note shall fill the earth again:
To God be glory! Peace, good will to men.[8]
      —Henry Robins

 Oh Haunting Spirit of the Ever True,
 Keep thou the pressure of Thy way upon us.
 We see a world too big to grasp;
 We glimpse a city too far off to reach;
 We trudge a way too long to walk;
 We feel a truth too pure to understand,
 We have a purpose that we cannot prove;
 A life to live beyond the power of living;
 A vision time or energy cannot contain;
 But faith that all our effort will not be in vain.

Oh, Haunting Spirit of the Ever True,
Keep thou the pressure of Thy way upon us.[9]
—Allan Chalmers

I now make it my earnest prayer
that God would have you,
and the state over which you preside, in His holy
    protection;
that He would incline the hearts of the citizens
to cultivate a spirit of subordination and obedience to
    the government;
to entertain a brotherly affection and love for one
    another,
for their fellow citizens of the United States at large
and particularly for their brethren who have served in
    the field;
and finally that He would graciously be pleased to dis-
    pose us all to do justice,
to love mercy, and to demean ourselves with charity
    and humility,
and a pacific temper of mind, which were characteris-
    tics of
the Divine Author of our blessed religion,
and without an humble imitation of whose example
    in these things,
we can never hope to be a happy nation.[10]
—George Washington

We always thank God, the Father of our Lord Jesus Christ, when we pray for you, because we have heard of your faith in Christ Jesus and of the love you have for all the saints—the faith and love that spring from the hope that is stored up for you in heaven and that you have already heard about in the word of truth, the gospel that has come to you. . . .

Since the day we heard about you, we have not stopped praying for you and asking God to fill you with the knowl-edge of his will through all spiritual wisdom and understand-

ing. And we pray this in order that you may live a life worthy of the Lord and may please him in every way: bearing fruit in every good work, growing in the knowledge of God, being strengthened with all power according to his glorious might so that you may have great endurance and patience, and joyfully giving thanks to the Father, who has qualified you to share in the inheritance of the saints in the kingdom of light.

—Paul, the apostle
Colossians 1:3–12 NIV

Lord, behold our family here assembled;
We thank Thee for this place in which we dwell,
    For the love that unites us,
    For the peace accorded us this day
    For the hope with which we expect the morrow
    For the health, the work, the food, and the bright skies
        that make our lives delightful
    For our friends in all parts of the earth . . .
Give us courage and gaiety and the quiet mind—
    Bless us if it may be in all our innocent endeavors
    If it may not, give us the strength to encounter
    That which is to come, that we may be brave in peril,
        constant in tribulation, temperate in wrath.
    And in all changes of fortune and down to the gate of
        death
    Loyal and loving to one another.
As the clay to the potter
As the windmill to the wind
As children of their sire—
    We beseech of Thee this help and mercy
    For Christ's sake.[11]

—Robert Louis Stevenson

Dear Jesus,
Please heal my mommie.
She has a cold
all the way down
to her heart.[12]
　　　　—Carrie [age 4]

Take Thou the burden, Lord;
I am exhausted with this heavy load.
　My tired hands tremble,
And I stumble, stumble
　Along the way.
Oh, lead with Thine unfailing arm
　Again today.

Unless Thou lead me, Lord,
The road I journey is all too hard
　Through trust in Thee alone
Can I go on.

Yet not for self alone
　Thus do I groan;
My people's sorrows are the load I bear.
　Lord, hear my prayer—
May Thy strong hand
　Strike off all chains
That load my well-loved land.
　God, draw her close to Thee![13]
　　　　—Toyohiko Kagawa

A missionary in Japan, Toyohiko's great ministry among the poor
lives on.

Give us, O God, the vision which can see thy love in the world
in spite of human failure. Give us the faith to trust thy goodness in spite of our ignorance and weakness. Give us the knowledge that we may continue to pray with understanding hearts,

and show us what each one of us can do to set forward the
coming of the day of universal peace.[14]

       —Frank Borman, Bill Anders, James Lovell

This prayer was the first uttered by astronauts from space.

> O God of earth and altar,
> Bow down and hear our cry,
> Our earthly rulers falter,
> Our people drift and die;
> The walls of gold entomb us,
> The swords of scorn divide,
> Take not thy thunder from us,
> But take away our pride.
>
> From all that terror teaches,
> From lies of tongue and pen,
> From all the easy speeches
> That comfort cruel men,
> From sale and profanation
> Of honor and the sword,
> From sleep and from damnation,
> Deliver us, good Lord!
>
> Tie in a living tether
> The prince and priest and thrall,
> Bind all our lives together,
> Smite us and save us all;
> In ire and exultation
> Aflame with faith, and free,
> Lift up a living nation
> A single sword to thee.[15]

       —G. K. Chesterton

Holy Child, whom the shepherds and the kings and the dumb
beasts adored, be born again. Wherever there is boredom,
wherever there is fear of failure, wherever there is bitterness of
heart, come, thou blessed one, with healing in thy wings.

Savior, be born in each of us who raises his face to thy face, not knowing fully who he is or who Thou art, knowing only that thy love is beyond his knowing and that no other has the power to make him whole. Come, Lord Jesus, to each who longs for thee, even though he has forgotten thy name. Come quickly. Amen.[16]

—Frederich Buechner

Dear God, The other day we were given a glimpse of boyhood memories from one of our guests. We had been talking about how Hitler had mesmerized the people so they didn't know what was going on: the death trains to Auschwitz, the inferno of Dachau, the elimination from society of the mentally ill and the aged and the sick.

This friend, Lord, then told us of a memory that haunted him. He said he was ten years old when he became a part of the Hitler Youth. It was the patriotic thing to do, and all his buddies were in it.

One day the old Catholic priest was coming out of the church as this sizable group of boys came marching down the street. The priest was so old and frail that he had to hold onto a rail when he turned. The leader ordered the boys to surround the priest and imprison him in their circle. Then they belittled and poked fun at him. The friend said he knew he should have refused to be a part of such sadistic cruelty, but he wasn't strong enough.

He never told us what became of the priest, but he said that all through the years he has been haunted by that memory. In spite of great musical gifts, he has never been able to find himself. . . . God, he needs you to heal his memories and it is only you who can do it.

As we bring to you our ugly remembrances, the times we've been cowardly and thoughtless, and ask forgiveness, you give us the promise of remembering no more. I plead for that, Lord, for the people I know who are haunted by the ghosts of past mistakes and lost opportunities.

Help us to take each day as a new beginning and not let the devil immobilize with unforgiven remorse. Thank you![17]
—Ruth Youngdahl Nelson

As I think of this great plan I fall on my knees before the Father (from whom all fatherhood, earthly or heavenly, derives its name), and I pray that out of the glorious richness of his resources he will enable you to know the strength of the Spirit's inner re-inforcement—that Christ may actually live in your hearts by your faith. And I pray that you, rooted and founded in love yourselves, may be able to grasp (with all Christians) how wide and long and deep and high is the love of Christ— and to know for yourselves that love so far above our understanding. So will you be filled through all your being with God himself!

Now to him who by his power within us is able to do infinitely more than we ever dare to ask or imagine—to him be glory in the Church and in Christ Jesus for ever and ever, amen!
—Paul, the apostle
Ephesians 3:14–21 PHILLIPS

Dear Lord,
My mother has a bad headache again today.
Can you help her with her headache?
When she has a headache, she is in a bad mood
and then my father gets a headache, too.[18]
Joseph [age 9]

O God, you know how those Aucas killed our beloved Señor Eduardo, Señor Jaime, and Señor Pedro. O God, you know that it was only because they did not know you. They did not know what a great sin it was. They did not understand why the white men had come. Send some more messengers, and give the Aucas, instead of fierce hearts, soft hearts. Stick their hearts, Lord, as with a lance. They stuck our friends, but you can stick them with your Word, so that they will listen and believe.[19]
—Quichua Indian Christians

Before being martyred by the Aucas, Ed McCully, Jim Elliot, and Pete Fleming had evangelized the Quichua tribe.

> God give us heroes! A time like this demands
> Strong minds, great hearts, true faith and ready hands;
> Those whom the lust of office does not kill;
> Those whom the spoils of office cannot buy;
> Those who possess opinions and a will;
> Those who have honor—those who will not lie;
> Those who can stand before a demagogue
> And damn his treacherous flatteries without winking;
> Tall folks, sun-crowned, who live above the fog
> In public duty and in private thinking;
> For while the rabble, with their thumb-worn creeds,
> Their large professions and their little deeds,
> Mingle in selfish strife, lo! Freedom weeps,
> Wrong rules the land and waiting Justice sleeps.[20]
>
> —Josiah Holland (adapted)

Father, the time has come. Glorify your Son, that your Son may glorify you. For you granted him authority over all people that he might give eternal life to all those you have given him. Now this is eternal life: that they may know you, the only true God, and Jesus Christ, whom you have sent. I have brought you glory on earth by completing the work you gave me to do. And now, Father, glorify me in your presence with the glory I had with you before the world began.

I have revealed you to those whom you gave me out of the world. They were yours; you gave them to me and they have obeyed your word. Now they know that everything you have given me comes from you. For I gave them the words you gave me and they accepted them. They knew with certainty that I came from you, and they believed that you sent me. I pray for them. I am not praying for the world, but for those you have given me, for they are yours. All I have is yours, and all you have is mine. And glory has come to me through them. I will remain in the world no longer, but they are still in the world, and I am coming to you. Holy Father, protect them by the power of your name—the name you gave me—so that they may be one as we are one. While I was with them, I protected them and kept them safe by that name you gave me. None has been lost except the one doomed to destruction so that Scripture would be fulfilled.

I am coming to you now, but I say these things while I am still in the world, so that they may have the full measure of my joy within them. I have given them your word and the world has hated them, for they are not of the world any more than I am of the world. My prayer is not that you take them out of the world but that you protect them from the evil one. They are not of the world, even as I am not of it. Sanctify them by the truth; your word is truth. As you sent me into the world, I have sent them into the world. For them I sanctify myself, that they too may be truly sanctified.

My prayer is not for them alone. I pray also for those who will believe in me through their message, that all of them may be one, Father, just as you are in me and I am in you. May they also be in us so that the world may believe that you have sent me. I have given them the glory that you gave me, that they may be one as we are one: I in them and you in me. May they be brought to complete unity to let the world know that you sent me and have loved them even as you have loved me.

Father, I want those you have given me to be with me where I am, and to see my glory, the glory you have given me because you loved me before the creation of the world.

—Jesus Christ
John 17 NIV

Grant, O merciful God, that with malice towards none, with charity for all, with firmness in the right as you give us to see the right, we may strive to finish the work we are in; to bind up the nation's wounds . . . to do all which may achieve and cherish a just and lasting peace among ourselves and with all nations through Jesus Christ our Lord.[21]

—Abraham Lincoln

Lord, save us from being self-centred in our prayers and teach us to remember to pray for others. May we be so bound up in love with those for whom we pray that we may feel their needs as acutely as our own and intercede for them with sensitivity, with understanding, and with imagination. We ask this in Christ's name.[22]

—John Calvin

14

Miscellaneous Unusual Prayers

Dear God, be good to me. The sea is so wide, and my boat is so small.[1]

—Breton fisherman's prayer

O God, I give you thanks
   that I am not like him
   sniveling there in the back row,
   bending beneath the weight of his woe.
I come to you with clean hands
   and a perfect record
   of fasting and giving
   and righteous living.
Examine my spiritual progress;
   find nothing amiss,
   an open book eager for your perusal,
   ready and waiting for your approval.
Probe my thoughts,
   the essence of my being,
   my motives, intentions,
   my honorable mentions.

Mighty Father, do you turn away from the radiance of my repute?
  Surely Omnipotence can reply
  to another sun in the sky.
Look not upon that figure in the shadows,
  those rounded shoulders
  shaking in self-accusation,
  meant to elicit consolation.
He is not one of us, Lord,
  not a star serenely set in heaven
  but a victim of dereliction
  fallen on the path to perfection.
Rather, see me in my splendor;
  let your majesty be mirrored,
  wisdom, power full returned,
  in the holiness I've earned.
O Judge most just, your attention to the front seat, please,
  to your servant so obedient,
  to the jots and tittles in my purse,
  to the list of prayers that I rehearse.
Pay no heed to sighs behind us,
  the gasp of guilt escaping
  lips pressed upon the back of the pew
  ratcheting out Psalm Twenty-two.
Against the blinding coalescence of our light,
  you can barely see the red-stained palms
  or the threadbare purple robe
  of one more bleakly faithful Job.
Not our kind at all, Lord,
  still, I will forgive your obvious distraction
  and join you in majestically expressing
  our deep concern in brief but heartfelt blessing.[2]

—Roger Swenson

Dear God
I like the Lord's prayer best of all.
Did you have to write it a lot or
did you get it right the first time?
I have to write everything
I ever write
over again.[3]

—Lois (child)

Come down, O Christ, and help me! Reach thy hand
For I am drowning in a stormier sea
Than Simon on thy lake of Galilee:
The wine of life is spilt upon the sand,
My heart is as some famine-murdered land
When all good things have perished utterly,
And well I know my soul in Hell must lie
If I this night before God's throne should stand.
He sleeps, perchance, or rideth to the chase,
Like Baal, when his prophets howled the name
From morn til noon on Carmel's smitten height.
Nay, peace, I shall behold before the night,
The feet of brass, the robe more white than flame,
The wounded hands, the weary human face.[4]

—Oscar Wilde

Wilde lived an immoral lifestyle, but here he seems to be crying out for mercy. It is not known if he ever took Christianity seriously.

Dear God,
On Halloween I am going to
wear a Devil's costume.
Is that all right with you?[5]

—Marnie (child)

God, Give me strength. Please get me through this. Let me be the very best I can be under these pressures. Give me the power and then I'm outta here.[6]

> —Bruce Jenner
> (U.S. winner of Olympic decathlon)

Dear God, A lot of folks say there is too much rough stuff on TV and too much killing. I say there is too much rough stuff and killing in the Bible. Make my day.[7]

> —Derek [age 11]

> You take the pen
> and the lines dance.
> You take the flute
> and the notes shimmer.
> You take the brush
> and the colours sing.
> So all things have meaning and beauty
> in that space beyond time where you are.
> How, then, can I hold back anything from you?[8]
> —Dag Hammarskjold
> (former Secretary General
> of the United Nations)

> We read Thos. Edison made light.
> But in Sun. School they said You
> did it.
> I bet he stoled your idea.[9]
> Sincerly,
> Donna (child)

God, help me to think clearly here. Help me to be clear and help me evaluate the situation.[10]

> —Lou Holtz
> (former football coach
> for University of Notre Dame)

Dear Lord,
    I say prayers every night
        except when I have an upset stomach
        and I don't want to talk to
        anybody.[11]

           —Teddy [age 8]

Dear God, please help my little boy to play the part of a man in this infectious blood-poisoning of nations we call war. Give him the strength to hold fast to his little-boy dreams while all the forces of international evil seek to turn him into an efficient and deadly killer. And if thou dost decree that he shall not come back, then let his end be sudden and sharp and not like that of Thine only Son who hung for long hours on Calvary. Give him the inspiration to protect and preserve the lives of the men he commands. And please remember, God, that he is only nineteen and a Second Lieutenant of Infantry in the U.S. Army.[12]

           —Father's prayer for son
           in World War II (excerpted)

Dear God,
Maybe Cain and Abel would not kill each other
so much if they had their own rooms.
It works with my brother.[13]

           —Larry (child)

Okay, I don't know if there's anybody out there listening, but I'm trying to do the right thing finally and I'm having a terrible time with this. So, I'm not going to ask for things because I've had things. I need some strength. I don't want anything material and I don't even ask for success. I just want more strength so I can do this one thing.[14]

           —David Crosby

Crosby was a former rhythm guitarist for the Byrds and for Crosby, Stills, Nash, and Young. He offered up this prayer during his battle to overcome an alcohol addiction.

Dear God,
How is it in heaven?
How is it being the Big Cheese?[15]
                    —Tom (child)

Lord! Where was I?
Oh yes! This flower, this sun,
thank you! Your world is beautiful.
This scent of roses. . . .
Where was I?
A drop of dew
rolls to sparkle in a lily's heart.
I have to go. . . .
Where? I do not know.
The wind has painted fancies
on my wings.
Fancies . . .
Where was I? Oh yes, Lord,
I had something to tell you—
Amen.[16]
                    —Carmen Gasztold
              (prayer of the butterfly)

Deer Lord,

  I am saying my prayers for me and my brother Billy because Billy is 6 months old and he can't do anything but sleep
and wet his diapers.[17]

                              Yours truly,
                              Diane [age 8]

Sanctify this milk that has been pressed into cheese, and press
us together in charity. Grant that this fruit of the olive tree
may never lose its savour; for the olive is a symbol of that
abundance which, at your bidding, flowed from the tree and
is there for those who trust you.[18]

                    —Blessing of Cheese and Olives
                 (second- or third-century church)

From Witches, Warlocks, and Worricoes,
From Ghoulies, Ghosties, and Long-leggit Beasties,
From all Things that go bump in the night—
Good Lord, deliver us.[19]
—Traditional Cornish prayer

God, I don't know what's going on. I really don't. Whoever is out there, I can't understand this. But thanks for protecting my home and my family. Give me strength from the air that I breathe and the earth that I walk upon.[20]
—Rod Steiger (actor)

Dear God,
I am doing
the best I can.[21]
—Frank (child)

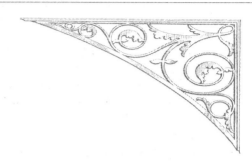

Epilogue

We hope you have found this collection encouraging, challenging, and even a little amusing at times. Many of these prayers have been prayed by some of the most holy and spiritually mature saints in history. We trust that you will find in them words to grow by. Spiritual growth can be much enhanced by learning from the greats.

We also invite you to pray some of the prayers yourself. Many times when euphoric with gratefulness or struggling with disappointment, words fail us, and we search for expression of our true emotions. There may be prayers in this book that you can make your own and can pray in such moments.

As you pray each day, may you sense God's immense pleasure in your prayers, whether they are halting, eloquent, fervent, or joyous.

—

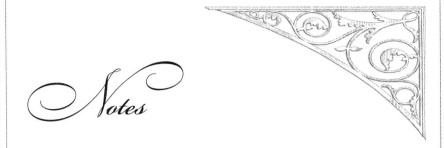

Chapter 1: Prayers in Crisis

1. Catherine Davis, ed., *Talking with God* (Colorado Springs: Chariot Victor, 1997), 72.
2. Peter Marshall, *The Prayers of Peter Marshall* (New York: McGraw Hill, 1954), 175.
3. Robert Van De Weyer, *The Harper-Collins Book of Prayers* (San Francisco: HarperSanFrancisco, 1993), 321.
4. Desmond Tutu, ed., *The African Prayer Book* (New York: Doubleday, 1995), 86–87.
5. Veronica Zundel, comp., *Eerdmans' Book of Famous Prayers* (Grand Rapids: Eerdmans, 1983), 44.
6. Sir Francis Drake, (source unknown).
7. Taken from *Incredible Moments with the Savior* by Ken Gire Jr. Copyright © 1990 by Ken Gire. Used by permission of Zondervan Publishing House.
8. Mary Batchelor, comp., *The Doubleday Prayer Collection* (New York: Doubleday, 1992), 13.
9. Richard Halverson, *No Greater Power: Perspective for Days of Pressure* (Portland, Ore.: Multnomah, 1986), 141–42.
10. Jacob Astley Baron, (source unknown).
11. Kefa Sempangi, *A Distant Grief* (Glendale, Calif.: Regal Books, 1979), 120–21.
12. Joan Brown, *The Martyred Christian* (New York: Macmillan, 1983), 171.
13. Halverson, *No Greater Power*, 63.

14. Children's prayer, (source unknown).

15. Thea Halsema, *Glorious Heretic: The Story of Guido de Bres* (Grand Rapids: Baker, 1991), 129.

16. Tutu, *The African Prayer Book*, 72–73.

17. Ruth Youngdahl Nelson, *A Grandma's Letters to God* (Minneapolis: Augsburg, 1983), 51–52.

Chapter 2: Prayers of Praise and Worship

1. Desmond Tutu, ed., *The African Prayer Book* (New York: Doubleday, 1995), 7–8.

2. Arthur Wortman, ed., *Springs of Devotion* (Kansas City: Hallmark Editions, 1969), 50.

3. Frederick W. Lewis, *Prayers That Are Different* (Grand Rapids: Eerdmans, 1964), 129.

4. A. W. Tozer, *The Christian Book of Mystical Verse* (Camp Hill, Pa.: Christian Publications, 1963), 79–81.

5. Mary Wilder Tileston, comp., *Daily Strength for Daily Needs* (New York: Grosset and Dunlap, 1884), 258.

6. Tutu, *The African Prayer Book*, n.p.

7. Veronica Zundel, comp., *Eerdmans' Book of Famous Prayers* (Grand Rapids: Eerdmans, 1983), 86.

8. Humphrey Milford, ed., *The English Hymnal* (London: A. B. Mowbray and Co., 1906), 375–76.

9. Tony Castle, ed., *The New Book of Christian Prayers* (New York: Crossroad, 1986), 205.

10. Mary Tileston, ed., *Joy and Strength* (Minneapolis: World Wide Publications, 1901), 191.

11. Tileston, *Daily Strength for Daily Needs*, 207.

12. Milford, *The English Hymnal*, 501–2.

13. Alexander Solzhenitsyn, *Solzhenitsyn: A Pictorial Autobiography* (New York: Farrar, Strauss and Giroux, 1974), n.p. Solzhenitsyn stated that this prayer was circulated in Russia in secret before it was published in the U.S.

14. Charles Wesley, "Jesus, Lover of My Soul," in *Hymns and Sacred Poems* (n.p., 1740), n.p.

15. Charles Fuller and Elwin Wright, eds., *Manna in the Morning* (Boston, Mass.: Fellowship Press, 1943), 211.

16. Tozer, *The Christian Book of Mystical Verse*, 7–8.

17. Tileston, *Daily Strength for Daily Needs*, 21.

18. Stuart and Jill Briscoe, comps., *The Family Book of Christian Values* (Colorado Springs: Chariot Books, 1995), 193.

19. Myrna Reid Grant, comp., *Poems for a Good and Happy Life* (Garden City, N.Y.: CrossAmerica Books, 1997), 228.

20. Shawn McGarry, ed., *A Woman's Book of Faith* (Secausus, N.J.: Carol Publications, 1997), 51.

21. Patricia Baxter, unpublished prayer. Used by permission.

22. Tileston, *Joy and Strength*, 180.

23. Stuart Hample and Eric Marshall, comps., *Children's Letters to God* (New York: Workman Publishers, 1991), n.p.

24. William Cowper, "Longing to Be with Christ," in *The Country of the Risen King: An Anthology of Christian Poetry*, comp. Merle Meeter (Grand Rapids: Baker, 1978), 306.

25. Tileston, *Daily Strength for Daily Needs*, 19.

26. *The Hymnal* (published by authority of the General Assembly of the Presbyterian Church in the United States of America, 1933), n.p.

Chapter 3: Prayers of Surrender

1. Jill Briscoe, *Hush! Hush!* (Grand Rapids: Zondervan, 1978), 122–23.

2. Cited in *Pen Power*, May 1995 (published by Chisholm Elementary School, Edmond, Okla.).

3. Frederick W. Lewis, *Prayers That Are Different* (Grand Rapids: Eerdmans, 1964), 299.

4. Corrie ten Boom, *Each New Day* (Old Tappan, N.J.: Revell, 1977), 151.

5. Veronica Zundel, comp., *Eerdmans' Book of Famous Prayers* (Grand Rapids: Eerdmans, 1983), 113.

6. This prayer is considered by some as originating with Reinhold Niebuhr, but Friedrich Christoph, a pastor, apparently wrote it in 1782. See David Redding, ed., *The Prayers I Love* (San Francisco: Strawberry Hill Press, 1978), n.p.

7. Mary Wilder Tileston, comp., *Daily Strength for Daily Needs* (New York: Grosset and Dunlap, 1884), 44.

8. Dietrich Bonhoeffer, *Letters and Papers from Prison* (New York: Collier, 1972), n.p.

9. James Morrison, ed., *Masterpieces of Religious Verse* (New York: Harper and Brothers, 1948), 576–77.

10. Arnold Dallimore, ed., *Spurgeon* (Chicago: Moody, 1984), 23.

11. Harry Emerson Fosdick, *The Meaning of Prayer* (New York: Association Press, 1916), n.p. Lady Jane Grey, an English noblewoman, was beheaded at age seventeen, as being a possible rival for the throne.

12. Emile Cailliet and John Blankenagel, trans., *Great Shorter Works of Pascal* (Philadelphia: Westminster, 1948), 220–21.

13. Carl Sandburg, *Lincoln's Devotional* (1852; reprint, New York: Henry Holt, 1995), 151.

14. Morrison, *Masterpieces of Religious Verse*, 558.

15. S. L. Greenslade, ed., *The Work of William Tyndale* (London: Blackie and Sons, 1938), n.p.

16. N. Habel, ed., *For Mature Adults Only* (Philadelphia: Fortress, 1969), 33–34.

17. Edith Deen, *Great Women of the Christian Faith* (New York: Harper and Brothers, 1959), 126–27.

18. Morrison, *Masterpieces of Religious Verse*, 75.

19. Mark Noll, ed., *Voices from the Heart* (Grand Rapids: Eerdmans, 1987), 9.

20. Zundel, *Eerdman's Book of Famous Prayers*, 61.

21. Deen, *Great Women of the Christian Faith*, 166.

Chapter 4: Prayers of Thanksgiving

1. James Morrison, ed., *Masterpieces of Religious Verse* (New York: Harper and Brothers, 1948), 345.

2. *Prayers Ancient and Modern* (New York: Grosset and Dunlap, 1897), 9.

3. Marjorie Holmes, *Hold Me Up a Little Longer, Lord* (New York: Doubleday, 1977), 65.

4. Catherine Davis, ed., *Talking with God* (Colorado Springs: Chariot Victor, 1997), 46.

5. Martha Whitmore Hickman, ed., *Prayers and Devotions for Teachers* (Nashville: Abingdon, 1989), 64.

6. Johnny Farese, unpublished prayer. Used by permission.

7. Morrison, *Masterpieces of Religious Verse*, 121.

8. Gert Behanna, *God Is Not Dead* (Richmond, Tex.: Well-Spring Center, 1977), n.p.

9. John Baille, *A Diary of Private Prayer* (New York: Charles Scribner's Sons, 1949), 25.

10. Morrison, *Masterpieces of Religious Verse*, 123.

11. Mel White, *Margaret of Molokai* (Waco, Tex.: Word, 1981), 185–86.

12. Anthony C. Fortosis, *Til We Meet Again* (self-published, 1982), 36. Used by permission.

13. William Kadel, *Prayers for Every Need* (Richmond: John Knox, 1963), 86.

Chapter 5: Prayers for Spiritual Growth

1. Peter Marshall, *The Prayers of Peter Marshall*, (New York: McGraw Hill, 1954), 15.

2. John Donne, selection found in untitled reference work of familiar quotations.

3. Keith Miller, *Habitation of Dragons* (Waco, Tex.: Word, 1970), 18.

4. Arthur Wortman, ed., *Springs of Devotion* (Kansas City: Hallmark Editions, 1969), 51–52.

5. Joyce Rupp, *Praying Our Goodbyes* (Notre Dame: Ave Maria, 1988), 135.

6. Bryan Jeffrey Leech, ed., *Hymns for the Family of God* (Nashville: Paragon Associates, 1976), 482.

7. Wortman, *Springs of Devotion*, 54.

8. Charles Fuller and Elwin Wright, eds., *Manna in the Morning* (Boston, Mass.: Fellowship Press, 1943), 9.

9. John L. Sandlin, *A Prayer for Every Day* (Westwood, N.J.: Revell, 1958), 23.

10. Arthur Bennett, ed., *The Valley of Vision: A Collection of Puritan Prayers and Devotions* (Carlisle, Pa.: Banner of Truth, 1975), 133.

11. Frederick W. Lewis, *Prayers That Are Different* (Grand Rapids: Eerdmans, 1964), 28.

12. Robertson McQuilkin, "Let Me Get Home Before Dark" (unpublished poem at this time). Used by permission. McQuilkin is President Emeritus at Columbia International University.

13. Bennett, *The Valley of Vision*, 110.

14. James Morrison, ed., *Masterpieces of Religious Verse* (New York: Harper and Brothers, 1948), 128.

15. Lissa Roche, ed., *The Christian's Treasury of Stories and Songs, Prayers and Poems and Much More for Young and Old* (Wheaton, Ill.: Crossway, 1995), 107.

16. Horton Davies, ed., *Communion of Saints: Prayers of the Famous* (Grand Rapids: Eerdmans, 1990), 47.

17. Morrison, *Masterpieces of Religious Verse*, 395.

18. Mary Batchelor, comp., *The Doubleday Prayer Collection* (New York: Doubleday, 1992), 12.

19. Stuart and Jill Briscoe, comps., *The Family Book of Christian Values* (Colorado Springs: Chariot Books, 1995), 130.

20. Davies, *Communion of Saints*, 84.

21. Bennett, *The Valley of Vision*, 106.

22. Davies, *Communion of Saints*, 84.

23. David McCasland, *Oswald Chambers: Abandoned to God* (Grand Rapids: Discovery House, 1993), 35.

24. Tony Castle, ed., *The New Book of Christian Prayers* (New York: Crossroad, 1986), 214–15.

25. Lewis, *Prayers That Are Different*, 123–24.

26. Castle, *The New Book of Christian Prayers*, 171.

27. Shawn McGarry, ed., *A Woman's Book of Faith* (Secaucus, N.J.: Carol Publications, 1997), 49.

28. Mary Wilder Tileston, comp., *Daily Strength for Daily Needs* (New York: Grosset and Dunlap, 1884), 116.

29. Roger Swenson, *Prayer and Remembrance* (Notre Dame: Ave Maria, 1989), 178.

30. Morrison, *Masterpieces of Religious Verse*, 227.

31. Andrew Murray, *The Believer's School of Prayer* (Minneapolis: Bethany House, 1982), 41.

32. Briscoe, *The Family Book of Christian Values*, 284.

33. John Baille, *A Diary of Private Prayer* (New York: Charles Scribner's Sons, 1949), 53, 73, 91.

34. Taken from *Incredible Moments with the Savior* by Ken Gire Jr. Copyright © 1990 by Ken Gire. Used by permission of Zondervan Publishing House.

35. Traditional prayer cited in *The Book of Common Worship* (approved by the General Assembly of the Presbyterian Church in the United States of America, Philadelphia, 1946).

36. Roche, *The Christian's Treasury*, 105.

37. Swenson, *Prayer and Remembrance*, 79–80.

38. Lewis, *Prayers That Are Different*, 156.

39. Morrison, *Masterpieces of Religious Verse*, 369.

40. Marshall, *The Prayers of Peter Marshall*, 51.

41. Rudyard Kipling, *Rudyard Kipling's Verse* (New York: Doubleday, 1940), n.p.

42. Cited in *The Book of Common Prayer*.

43. George Herbert, "Easter Wings," in *The Country of the Risen King: An Anthology of Christian Poetry*, comp. Merle Meeter (Grand Rapids: Baker, 1978), 327.

44. Bennett, *The Valley of Vision*, 165.

45. Morrison, *Masterpieces of Religious Verse*, 409.

46. Swenson, *Prayer and Remembrance*, 184–85.

47. Murray, *The Believers' School of Prayer*, 26–27.

48. Myrna Reid Grant, comp., *Poems for a Good and Happy Life* (Garden City, N.Y.: CrossAmerica Books, 1997), 99.

Chapter 6: Prayers of Questioning

1. David Heller, *The Children's God* (Chicago: University of Chicago, 1986), 39.
2. N. Habel, ed., *For Mature Adults Only* (Philadelphia: Fortress, 1969), 28–29.
3. Bill Adler, *Children's Letters to God* (New York: Little, Brown, and Co., n.d.), n.p.
4. Children's prayer, (source unknown).
5. James Morrison, ed., *Masterpieces of Religious Verse* (New York: Harper and Brothers, 1948), 225.
6. Stuart Hample and Eric Marshall, comps., *Children's Letters to God* (New York: Workman Publishers, 1991), n.p.
7. Mary Rose McGeady, *Are You Out There, God?* (self-published, 1996), 21.
8. Hample and Marshall, *Children's Letters to God*, n.p.
9. Cheri Fuller, *When Children Pray* (Sisters, Ore.: Multnomah, 1998), 16.
10. Hample and Marshall, *Children's Letters to God*, n.p.
11. Habel, *For Mature Adults Only*, 54–55.
12. Hample and Marshall, *Children's Letters to God*, n.p.
13. Ruth Harms Calkin, *Lord, It Keeps Happening . . . and Happening* (Wheaton: Tyndale House, 1984), 86–87.
14. Hample and Marshall, *Children's Letters to God*, n.p.
15. Ibid.
16. Habel, *For Mature Adults Only*, 69–70.
17. Adler, *Children's Letters to God*, n.p.
18. Heller, *The Children's God*, 105.

Chapter 7: Prayers for Children

1. Ruth Graham, *Sitting by My Laughing Fire* (Minneapolis: World Wide Publications, 1977), 156.
2. Taken from *Prayers to Pray Without Really Trying* by Jeanette Struchen, 18. Copyright © 1967 by Jeanette Struchen. Reprinted by permission of HarperCollins Publishers, Inc.
3. Leon and Elfreda McCauley, eds., *The Book of Prayers* (New York: Crown Publishers, 1954), 163.
4. Marjorie Holmes, *Hold Me Up a Little Longer, Lord* (New York: Doubleday, 1977), 63–64, 101.
5. Bryan Jeffrey Leech, ed., *Hymns for the Family of God* (Nashville: Paragon Associates, 1976), 1976.

6. William Bennett, ed., *The Book of Virtues* (New York: Simon and Schuster, 1993), 744.
7. Anonymous, (source unknown).
8. Martha Whitmore Hickman, ed., *Prayers and Devotions for Teachers* (Nashville: Abingdon, 1989), 73.
9. Micheal Elliott, *Partners in Grace: Friends of the Salty Saints* (Cleveland, Ohio: Pilgrim Press, 1992), 78–79
10. Hickman, *Prayers and Devotions for Teachers*, 69.
11. Holmes, *Hold Me Up a Little Longer, Lord*, 26.
12. Edith Schaeffer, ed., *The Life of Prayer* (Wheaton, Ill.: Crossway, 1992), 204.
13. Graham, *Sitting by My Laughing Fire*, 96.

Chapter 8: Prayers of Confession

1. Source unknown.
2. Mary Wilder Tileston, comp., *Daily Strength for Daily Needs* (New York: Grosset and Dunlap, 1884), 180.
3. Marjorie Holmes, *Hold Me Up a Little Longer, Lord* (New York: Doubleday, 1977), 31.
4. Tileston, *Daily Strength for Daily Needs*, 202.
5. Richard Halverson, *No Greater Power: Perspective for Days of Pressure* (Portland, Ore.: Multnomah, 1986), 23.
6. James Morrison, ed., *Masterpieces of Religious Verse* (New York: Harper and Brothers, 1948), 205.
7. Ruth Graham, *Sitting by My Laughing Fire* (Minneapolis: World Wide Publications, 1977), 142.
8. Micheal Elliott, *Partners in Grace: Friends of the Salty Saints* (Cleveland, Ohio: Pilgrim Press, 1992), 149.
9. Charles Wesley, (source unknown).
10. Bryan Jeffrey Leech, ed., *Hymns for the Family of God* (Nashville: Paragon Associates, 1976), 649.
11. Desmond Tutu, ed., *The African Prayer Book* (New York: Doubleday, 1995), 42.
12. Harry Emerson Fosdick, *The Meaning of Prayer* (New York: Association Press, 1916), n.p.
13. Anonymous, (source unknown).
14. Mary Batchelor, comp., *The Doubleday Prayer Collection* (New York: Doubleday, 1992), 50–51.
15. John Baille, *A Diary of Private Prayer* (New York: Charles Scribner's Sons, 1949), 75.

16. Tony Castle, ed., *The New Book of Christian Prayers* (New York: Crossroad, 1986), 171.
17. Morrison, *Masterpieces of Religious Verse*, 297.
18. Castle, *The New Book of Christian Prayers*, 74.
19. Keith Green, *No Compromise* (Chatsworth, Calif.: Sparrow, 1989), 162.
20. Veronica Zundel, comp., *Eerdmans' Book of Famous Prayers* (Grand Rapids: Eerdmans, 1983), 45.
21. Stuart and Jill Briscoe, comps., *The Family Book of Christian Values* (Colorado Springs: Chariot Books, 1995), 66.
22. Peter Marshall, *The Prayers of Peter Marshall* (New York, McGraw Hill, 1954), 18.
23. Briscoe, *The Family Book of Christian Values*, 335–36.
24. Edith Schaeffer, ed., *The Life of Prayer* (Wheaton, Ill.: Crossway, 1992), 254.
25. Cited in *The Book of Common Prayer*.

Chapter 9: Prayers of Consecration

1. Gustav Konig, *Life of Martin Luther* (London: Nathaniel Cooke, 1853), 28.
2. Horton Davies, ed., *Communion of Saints: Prayers of the Famous* (Grand Rapids: Eerdmans, 1990), 20.
3. Garden Blaikie, *The Personal Life of David Livingstone* (New York: Laymen's Missionary Movement, 1910), 453.
4. James Morrison, ed., *Masterpieces of Religious Verse* (New York: Harper and Brothers, 1948), 75.
5. John Baille, *A Diary of Private Prayer* (New York: Charles Scribner's Sons, 1949), 41.
6. Bryan Jeffrey Leech, ed., *Hymns for the Family of God* (Nashville: Paragon Associates, 1976), 471.
7. Char Meredith, *It's a Sin to Bore a Kid* (Waco, Tex.: Word, 1978), 78.
8. Mary Wilder Tileston, comp., *Daily Strength for Daily Needs* (New York: Grosset and Dunlap, 1884), 361.
9. Taken from *Prayers to Pray Without Really Trying* by Jeanette Struchen, 52. Copyright © 1967 by Jeanette Struchen. Reprinted by permission of HarperCollins Publishers, Inc.
10. Myrna Reid Grant, comp., *Poems for a Good and Happy Life* (Garden City, N.Y.: CrossAmerica Books, 1997), 168.
11. Ibid., 172.
12. Ibid., 171.
13. Veronica Zundel, comp., *Eerdmans' Book of Famous Prayers* (Grand Rapids: Eerdmans, 1983), 39.

14. Jim Elliot, *The Journals of Jim Elliot,* ed. Elisabeth Elliot (Old Tappan, N.J.: Revell, 1978), 450.

15. Mary Tileston, ed., *Joy and Strength* (Minneapolis: World Wide Publications, 1901), 364.

16. Shawn McGarry, ed., *A Woman's Book of Faith* (Secausus, N.J.: Carol Publications, 1997), 31.

17. Leon and Elfreda McCauley, eds., *The Book of Prayers* (New York: Crown Publishers, 1954), 69.

18. A. W. Tozer, *The Christian Book of Mystical Verse* (Camp Hill, Pa.: Christian Publications, 1963), 73–74.

19. Mary Visscher, "The Way to Live," *The Church Herald,* 7 September 1979, 15.

20. Edith Schaeffer, ed., *The Life of Prayer* (Wheaton, Ill.: Crossway, 1992), 182.

21. Elizabeth Elliot, *Let Me Be a Woman* (Wheaton, Ill.: Tyndale House, 1976), n.p.

22. Morrison, *Masterpieces of Religious Verse,* 242.

23. *Prayers Ancient and Modern* (New York: Grosset and Dunlap, 1897), 52.

24. Tileston, *Joy and Strength,* 185.

25. Ruth Harms Calkin, *Lord, It Keeps Happening . . . and Happening* (Wheaton: Tyndale House, 1984), 103–4.

26. Tileston, *Joy and Strength,* 28.

27. Morrison, *Masterpieces of Religious Verse,* 112.

28. Stuart Hample and Eric Marshall, comps., *Children's Letters to God* (New York: Workman Publishers, 1991), n.p.

29. Charles Fuller and Elwin Wright, eds., *Manna in the Morning* (Boston, Mass.: Fellowship Press, 1943), 9.

30. Grant, *Poems for a Good and Happy Life,* 137.

31. Carl Sandburg, *Lincoln's Devotional* (1852; reprint, New York: Henry Holt, 1995), 124.

32. Fuller and Wright, *Manna in the Morning,* 21.

33. Ibid., 168.

34. Sandburg, *Lincoln's Devotional,* 122.

35. Morrison, *Masterpieces of Religious Verse,* 192.

Chapter 10: Prayers of and for Love and Kindness

1. Micheal Elliott, *Partners in Faith: Friends of the Salty Saints* (Cleveland: Pilgrim Press, 1992), 138.

2. William Kadel, *Prayers for Every Need* (Richmond: John Knox, 1963), 152.

3. Robert Van De Weyer, *The Harper-Collins Book of Prayers* (San Francisco: HarperSanFrancisco, 1993), 396.

4. Lissa Roche, ed., *The Christian's Treasury of Stories and Songs, Prayers and Poems and Much More for Young and Old* (Wheaton, Ill.: Crossway, 1995), 106.

5. Frederick Ohler, *Better Than Nice and Other Unconventional Prayers* (Louisville, Ky.: Westminster, 1989), 30.

6. Roche, *The Christian's Treasury*, 110.

7. Walter Wangerin, *Ragman and Other Cries of Faith* (San Francisco: HarperSanFrancisco, 1984), 7–8.

8. *Prayers Ancient and Modern* (New York: Grosset and Dunlap, 1897), 298.

9. Carl Sandburg, *Lincoln's Devotional* (1852; reprint, New York: Henry Holt, 1995), 126.

10. William Barclay, *More Prayers for the Plain Man* (London: Fontana Books, 1962), 98.

11. Richard Rolle, "Develop in Me a Longing That Is Unrestrained," in *Prayers from the Heart*, ed. Richard J. Foster (New York: HarperCollins, 1994), 52.

12. *Prayers Ancient and Modern*, 40.

13. Leon and Elfreda McCauley, eds., *The Book of Prayers* (New York: Crown Publishers, 1954), 29.

14. Arthur Bennett, ed., *The Valley of Vision: A Collection of Puritan Prayers and Devotions* (Carlisle, Pa.: Banner of Truth, 1975), 183.

15. Charles Fuller and Elwin Wright, eds., *Manna in the Morning* (Boston, Mass.: Fellowship Press, 1943), 59.

16. Andrew Murray, *The Believer's School of Prayer* (Minneapolis: Bethany House, 1982), 172–73.

17. Barclay, *More Prayers for the Plain Man*, 157.

18. Stuart Hample and Eric Marshall, comps., *Children's Letters to God* (New York: Workman Publishers, 1991), n.p.

19. John Lloyd Ogilvie, *Let God Love You* (Waco, Tex.: Word, 1974), n.p.

20. Veronica Zundel, comp., *Eerdmans' Book of Famous Prayers* (Grand Rapids: Eerdmans, 1983), 77.

21. Zundel, *Eerdman's Book of Famous Prayers*, 41.

22. Sandburg, *Lincoln's Devotional*, 4.

Chapter 11: Prayers for Enlightenment and Spiritual Intimacy

1. James Morrison, ed., *Masterpieces of Religious Verse* (New York: Harper and Brothers, 1948), n.p.

2. David Heller, *The Children's God* (Chicago: University of Chicago, 1986), 39.

3. Morrison, *Masterpieces of Religious Verse*, 238.

4. Ibid., 95.

5. Ibid., 67.

6. A. W. Tozer, *The Christian Book of Mystical Verse* (Camp Hill, Pa.: Christian Publications, 1963), 112.

7. Tozer, *The Christian Book of Mystical Verse*, 50.

8. N. Habel, ed., *For Mature Adults Only* (Philadelphia: Fortress, 1969), 17–18.

9. E. Cowman, comp., *Streams in the Desert* (Grand Rapids: Zondervan, 1925), 273–74.

10. Frederick W. Lewis, *Prayers That Are Different* (Grand Rapids: Eerdmans, 1964), 162–64.

11. Roger Swenson, *Prayer and Remembrance* (Notre Dame: Ave Maria, 1989), 142–43.

12. Leon and Elfreda McCauley, eds., *The Book of Prayers* (New York: Crown Publishers, 1954), 97.

13. Morrison, *Masterpieces of Religious Verse*, 235.

14. Habel, *For Mature Adults Only*, 82–83.

15. Ruth Youngdahl Nelson, *A Grandma's Letters to God* (Minneapolis: Augsburg, 1983), 108–11.

16. Joyce Rupp, *Praying Our Goodbyes* (Notre Dame: Ave Maria, 1988), 140.

17. Tozer, *The Christian Book of Mystical Verse*, 104.

18. Lancelot Andrewes, *The Private Devotions of Lancelot Andrewes* (New York: Meridian Books, 1961), 192.

19. Martha Whitmore Hickman, ed., *Prayers and Devotions for Teachers* (Nashville: Abingdon, 1989), 84.

20. Shawn McGarry, ed., *A Woman's Book of Faith* (Secausus, N.J.: Carol Publications, 1997), 110.

21. Habel, *For Mature Adults Only*, 59–60.

22. Thomas à Kempis, *The Imitation of Christ* (New York: Pocket Books, 1954), 151–54.

Chapter 12: Prayers of Daily Petition

1. Elizabeth Yates, comp., *Your Prayers and Mine* (Boston: Houghton-Mifflin, 1954), 39.

2. Children's prayer, (source unknown).

3. Desmond Tutu, ed., *The African Prayer Book* (New York: Doubleday, 1995), 105.

4. Stuart Hample and Eric Marshall, comps., *Children's Letters to God* (New York: Workman Publishers, 1991), n.p.

5. Yates, *Your Prayers and Mine,* 36.

6. Mary Batchelor, comp., *The Doubleday Prayer Collection* (New York: Doubleday, 1992), 333.

7. Ralph Woods, ed., *A Third Treasury of the Familiar* (New York: Macmillan, 1970), n.p.

8. Micheal Elliott, *Partners in Love: Friends of the Salty Saints* (Cleveland, Ohio: Pilgrim Press, 1992), 78–79.

9. Hample and Marshall, *Children's Letters to God,* n.p.

10. Charles H. Spurgeon, *Our Own Hymnbook* (Pasadena, Tex.: Pilgrim Publications, 1975), 213.

11. Yates, *Your Prayers and Mine,* 31.

12. Micheal Elliott, *Partners in Grace: Friends of the Salty Saints,* 34.

13. Martha Whitmore Hickman, ed., *Prayers and Devotions for Teachers* (Nashville: Abingdon, 1989), 94.

14. Hample and Marshall, *Children's Letters to God,* n.p.

15. N. Habel, ed., *For Mature Adults Only* (Philadelphia: Fortress, 1969), 87–88.

16. A. J. Broomhall, *Strong Man's Prey* (London: China Inland Mission, 1953), 220–22.

17. Taken from *Prayers to Pray Without Really Trying* by Jeanette Struchen, 14. Copyright © 1967 by Jeanette Struchen. Reprinted by permission of HarperCollins Publishers, Inc.

18. David Heller, *The Children's God* (Chicago: University of Chicago, 1986), 149.

19. A prayer by an anonymous seventeenth-century nun, seen on a print without a listed source, which was purchased in a London bookstore.

20. Batchelor, *The Doubleday Prayer Collection,* 291.

21. Heller, *The Children's God,* 130.

22. Habel, *For Mature Adults Only,* 59–60.

23. William Barclay, *More Prayers for the Plain Man* (London: Fontana Books, 1962), 28.

24. Veronica Zundel, comp., *Eerdmans' Book of Famous Prayers* (Grand Rapids: Eerdmans, 1983), 19.

25. Hample and Marshall, *Children's Letters to God,* n.p.

26. Richard Halverson, *No Greater Power: Perspective for Days of Pressure* (Portland, Ore.: Multnomah, 1986), 51.

27. Anonymous, "Physician's Prayer," (unpublished source).

28. Taken from *Prayers to Pray Without Really Trying* by Jeanette Struchen,

50. Copyright © 1967 by Jeanette Struchen. Reprinted by permission of HarperCollins Publishers, Inc.

29. Thomas Tiplady, (source unknown).

30. Howard Thurman, "Lord, Lord, Open unto Me," in *Prayers from the Heart*, ed. Richard J. Foster (New York: HarperCollins, 1994), 31.

31. Ruth Harms Calkin, *Lord, It Keeps Happening . . . and Happening* (Wheaton: Tyndale House, 1984), 103–4.

32. Charles Fuller and Elwin Wright, eds., *Manna in the Morning* (Boston, Mass.: Fellowship Press, 1943), 71–72.

33. Heller, *The Children's God*, 94.

Chapter 13: Prayers of Intercession

1. Cheri Fuller, *When Children Pray* (Sisters, Ore.: Multnomah, 1998), 38.

2. Lissa Roche, ed., *The Christian's Treasury of Stories and Songs, Prayers and Poems and Much More for Young and Old* (Wheaton, Ill.: Crossway, 1995), 109.

3. Veronica Zundel, comp., *Eerdmans' Book of Famous Prayers* (Grand Rapids: Eerdmans, 1983), 57.

4. Richard Halverson, *No Greater Power: Perspective for Days of Pressure* (Portland, Ore.: Multnomah, 1986), 27.

5. Humphrey Milford, ed., *The English Hymnal* (London: A. B. Mowbray and Co., 1906), 467.

6. Roche, *The Christian's Treasury*, 117–18.

7. Cited in *The Book of Common Prayer*, based on Num. 6:24–26.

8. James Morrison, ed., *Masterpieces of Religious Verse* (New York: Harper and Brothers, 1948), 454–55.

9. Ibid., 232–33.

10. Myrna Reid Grant, comp., *Poems for a Good and Happy Life* (Garden City, N.Y.: CrossAmerica Books, 1997), 82.

11. Graham Balfour, *The Life of Robert Louis Stevenson*, vol. 2 (New York: Charles Scribner's Sons, 1901), n.p.

12. Fuller, *When Children Pray*, 49.

13. Morrison, *Masterpieces of Religious Verse*, 91.

14. Catherine Davis, ed., *Talking with God* (Colorado Springs: Chariot Victor, 1997), 87.

15. Milford, *The English Hymnal*, 485.

16. Frederick Buechner, *Listening to Your Life* (San Francisco: Harper SanFrancisco, 1992), 341.

17. Ruth Youngdahl Nelson, *A Grandma's Letters to God* (Minneapolis: Augsburg, 1983), 66–67.

18. *Children's prayer,* (source unknown).

19. Elizabeth Elliot, *Through Gates of Splendor* (New York: Harper and Row, 1958), 256.

20. Josiah Holland, (source unknown).

21. Horton Davies, ed., *Communion of Saints: Prayers of the Famous* (Grand Rapids: Eerdmans, 1990), 112.

22. Tony Castle, ed., *The New Book of Christian Prayers* (New York: Crossroad, 1986), 166.

Chapter 14: Miscellaneous Unusual Prayers

1. Veronica Zundel, comp., *Eerdmans' Book of Famous Prayers* (Grand Rapids: Eerdmans, 1983), 58.

2. Roger Swenson, *Prayer and Remembrance* (Notre Dame: Ave Maria, 1989), 45–46.

3. Bill Adler, *Children's Letters to God* (New York: Little, Brown, and Co., n.d.), n.p.

4. Myrna Reid Grant, comp., *Poems for a Good and Happy Life* (Garden City, N.Y.: CrossAmerica Books, 1997), 187.

5. Stuart Hample and Eric Marshall, comps., *Children's Letters to God* (New York: Workman Publishers, 1991), n.p.

6. Larry King, *Powerful Prayers* (Los Angeles: Renaissance Books, 1998), 165–66.

7. *Children's prayer,* (source unknown).

8. Zundel, *Eerdmans' Book of Famous Prayers,* 95.

9. Hample and Marshall, *Children's Letters to God,* n.p.

10. King, *Powerful Prayers,* 167–68.

11. Adler, *Children's Letters to God,* n.p.

12. King, *Powerful Prayers,* 207.

13. Hample and Marshall, *Children's Letters to God,* n.p.

14. King, *Powerful Prayers,* 90.

15. David Heller, *The Children's God* (Chicago: University of Chicago, 1986), 31.

16. Zundel, *Eerdman's Book of Famous Prayers,* 101.

17. Adler, *Children's Letters to God,* n.p.

18. Zundel, *Eerdman's Book of Famous Prayers,* 120.

19. Tony Castle, ed., *The New Book of Christian Prayers* (New York: Crossroad, 1986), 129.

20. King, *Powerful Prayers,* 48–49.

21. Hample and Marshall, *Children's Letters to God,* n.p.

Bibliography

Adler, Bill. *Children's Letters to God.* New York: Little, Brown, and Co., n.d.

à Kempis, Thomas. *The Imitation of Christ.* New York: Pocket Books, 1954.

Andrewes, Lancelot. *The Private Devotions of Lancelot Andrewes.* New York: Meridian Books, 1961.

Baille, John. *A Diary of Private Prayer.* New York: Charles Scribner's Sons, 1949.

Balfour, Graham. *The Life of Robert Louis Stevenson.* Vol. 2. New York: Charles Scribner's Sons, 1901.

Barclay, William. *More Prayers for the Plain Man.* London: Fontana Books, 1962.

Barker, Kenneth, ed. *niv Study Bible.* Grand Rapids: Zondervan, 1995.

Batchelor, Mary, comp. *The Doubleday Prayer Collection.* New York: Doubleday, 1992.

Behanna, Gert. *God Is Not Dead.* Richmond, Tex.: Well-Spring Center, 1977.

Bennett, Arthur, ed. *The Valley of Vision: A Collection of Puritan Prayers and Devotions.* Carlisle, Pa.: Banner of Truth, 1975.

Blaikie, Garden. *The Personal Life of David Livingstone.* New York: Laymen's Missionary Movement, 1910.

Bonhoeffer, Dietrich. *Letters and Papers from Prison.* New York: Collier, 1972.

Book of Common Worship. Approved by the General Assembly of the Presbyterian Church in the U.S.A., Philadelphia, 1946.

Briscoe, Jill. *Hush! Hush!* Grand Rapids: Zondervan, 1978.

Briscoe, Stuart and Jill, comps. *The Family Book of Christian Values.* Colorado Springs: Chariot Books, 1995.

Broomhall, A. J. *Strong Man's Prey.* London: China Inland Mission, 1953.

Brown, Joan, ed. *The Martyred Christian.* New York: Macmillan, 1983.

Caillet, Emile and John Blankenagel, trans. *Great Shorter Works of Blaise Pascal.* Philadelphia: Westminster, 1948.

Chapian, Mary, ed. *Feeling Small; Walking Tall.* Minneapolis: Bethany House, 1989.

Coffin, Charles, ed. *The Complete Poetry and Selected Prose of John Donne.* New York: Random House, 1952.

Cowman, E., comp. *Streams in the Desert.* Grand Rapids: Zondervan, 1925.

Cowper, William. "Longing to Be with Christ." In *The Country of the Risen King: An Anthology of Christian Poetry.* Comp. Merle Meeter. Grand Rapids: Baker, 1978.

Davies, Horton, ed. *Communion of Saints: Prayers of the Famous.* Grand Rapids: Eerdmans, 1990.

Davis, Catherine, ed. *Talking with God.* Colorado Springs: Chariot Victor, 1997.

Deen, Edith. *Great Women of the Christian Faith.* New York: Harper and Brothers, 1959.

DeJong, Benjamin, comp. *Uncle Ben's Quotebook.* Eugene, Ore.: Harvest House, 1976.

Elliot, Elizabeth. *Through Gates of Splendor.* New York: Harper and Row, 1958.

Fortosis, Anthony C. *Til We Meet Again.* Self-published, 1982.

Fosdick, Emerson Harry. *The Meaning of Prayer.* New York: Association Press, 1916.

Foster, Richard, ed. *Prayers from the Heart.* New York: HarperCollins, 1994.

Fuller, Charles, and Elwin Wright, eds., *Manna in the Morning.* Boston: Fellowship Press, 1943.

Gire, Ken. *Incredible Moments with the Savior.* Grand Rapids: Zondervan, 1990.

Graham, Ruth. *Sitting by My Laughing Fire.* Minneapolis: World Wide Publications, 1977.

Grant, Myrna Reid, comp. *Poems for a Good and Happy Life.* Garden City, N.Y.: CrossAmerica Books, 1997.

Green, Keith. *No Compromise.* Chatsworth, Calif.: Sparrow, 1989.

Greenslade, S. L., ed. *The Work of William Tyndale.* London: Blackie and Sons, 1938.

Habel, N., ed. *For Mature Adults Only.* Philadelphia: Fortress, 1969.

Halverson, Richard. *No Greater Power: Perspective for Days of Pressure.* Portland, Ore.: Multnomah, 1986.

Hample, Stuart, and Eric Marshall, comps. *Children's Letters to God.* New York: Workman Publishing, 1991.

Herbert, George. "Easter Wings." In *The Country of the Risen King: An Anthology of Christian Poetry.* Comp. Merle Meeter. Grand Rapids: Baker, 1978.

Hickman, Martha Whitmore. *Prayers and Devotions for Teachers.* Nashville: Abingdon, 1989.

Holmes, Marjorie. *Hold Me Up a Little Longer, Lord.* Garden City, N.Y.: Doubleday, 1977.

The Hymnal. Published by the authority of the General Assembly of the Presbyterian Church of the U.S.A., Philadelphia, 1933.

Kadel, William. *Prayers for Every Need.* Richmond: John Knox, 1957.

King, Larry. *Powerful Prayers.* Los Angeles: Renaissance, 1998.

Kipling, Rudyard. *Rudyard Kipling's Verse.* New York: Doubleday, 1940.

Konig, Gustav. *Life of Martin Luther.* London: Nathaniel Cooke, 1853.

Leech, Bryan Jeffrey, ed. *Hymns for the Family of God.* Nashville: Paragon Associates, 1976.

Lewis, Frederick W. *Prayers That Are Different.* Grand Rapids: Eerdmans, 1964.

Marshall, Peter. *The Prayers of Peter Marshall.* New York: McGraw Hill, 1954.

McCasland, David. *Oswald Chambers: Abandoned to God.* Grand Rapids: Discovery House, 1993.

McCauley, Leon and Elfreda, eds. *The Book of Prayers.* New York: Crown Publishers, 1954.

McGarry, Shawn, ed. *A Woman's Book of Faith.* Secausus, N.J.: Carol Publications, 1997.

McGeady, Mary Rose. *Are You Out There, God?* Self-published, 1996.

Meredith, Char. *It's a Sin to Bore a Kid.* Waco, Tex.: Word, 1978.

Milford, Humphrey, ed. *The English Hymnal.* London: A. B. Mowbray and Co., 1906.

Miller, Keith. *Habitation of Dragons.* Waco, Tex.: Word, 1970.

Milliken, Bill. *So Long, Sweet Jesus.* New York: Prometheus Press, 1973.

Morrison, James, ed. *Masterpieces of Religious Verse.* New York: Harper and Brothers, 1948.

Murray, Andrew. *The Believer's School of Prayer.* Minneapolis: Bethany House, 1982.

Nelson, Ruth Youngdahl. *A Grandma's Letters to God.* Minneapolis: Augsburg, 1983.

Ogilvie, John Lloyd. *Let God Love You.* Waco, Tex.: Word, 1974.

Ohler, Frederick. *Better Than Nice and Other Unconventional Prayers.* Louisville, Ky.: Westminster, 1989.

Pen Power, May 1995. Published by Chisholm Elementary School, Edmund, Okla.

Redding, David, ed. *The Prayers I Love.* San Francisco: Strawberry Hill Press, 1978.

Roche, Lissa, ed. *The Christian's Treasury of Stories and Songs, Prayers and Poems and Much More for Young and Old.* Wheaton, Ill.: Crossway, 1995.

Rolle, Richard. "Develop in Me a Longing That Is Unrestrained." In *Prayers from the Heart.* Ed. Richard J. Foster. New York: HarperCollins, 1994.

Rupp, Joyce. *Praying Our Goodbyes.* Notre Dame: Ave Maria, 1988.

Sandburg, Carl. *Lincoln's Devotional.* 1852. Reprint, New York: Henry Holt, 1995.

Sandlin, John L. *A Prayer for Every Day.* Westwood, N.J.: Revell, 1958.

Schaeffer, Edith, ed. *The Life of Prayer.* Wheaton, Ill.: Crossway, 1992.

Sempangi, Kefa. *A Distant Grief.* Glendale, Calif.: Regal Books, 1979.

Solzhenitsyn, Alexander. *Solzhenitsyn: A Pictorial Autobiography.* New York: Farrar, Strauss and Giroux, 1974.

Spurgeon, Charles H. *Our Own Hymnbook.* Pasadena, Tex.: Pilgrim Publications, 1975.

Swenson, Roger. *Prayer and Remembrance.* Notre Dame: Ave Maria, 1989.

Ten Boom, Corrie. *Each New Day.* Old Tappan, N.J.: Revell, 1977.

Teresa, Mother. *A Gift for God.* San Francisco: Harper and Row, 1975.

Thurman, Howard. "Lord, Lord, Open unto Me." In *Prayers from the Heart.* Ed. Richard J. Foster. New York: HarperCollins, 1994.

Tileston, Mary Wilder, ed. *Joy and Strength.* Minneapolis: World Wide Publications, 1901.

Tozer, A. W. *The Christian Book of Mystical Verse.* Camp Hill, Pa.: Christian Publications, 1963.

Tutu, Desmond, ed. *The African Prayer Book.* New York: Doubleday, 1995.

Van de Weyer, Robert, ed. *The Harper-Collins Book of Prayers.* San Francisco: HarperSanFrancisco, 1993.

Visscher, Mary. "The Way to Live." *The Church Herald,* 7 September 1979.

Vogue Magazine, Christmas issue, 1971.

Wangerin, Walter. *Ragman and Other Cries of Faith.* San Francisco: HarperSanFrancisco, 1984.

Wesley, Charles. *Hymns and Sacred Poems.* N.p., 1740.

Woods, Ralph, ed. *A Third Treasury of the Familiar.* New York: Macmillan, 1970.

Wortman, Arthur. *Springs of Devotion.* Kansas City: Hallmark Editions, 1969.

Yates, Elizabeth, comp. *Your Prayers and Mine.* Boston: Houghton-Mifflin, 1954.

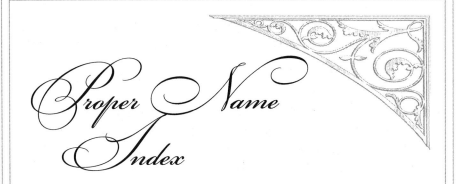

Proper Name Index